CHRIST, CULTURE, AND THE

AUTHENTIC
LOVE

D.A. HORTON

truelovewaits.

LifeWay Press® Nashville, Tennessee

ISBN: 978-1-4300-6458-9
Item 005791912

Dewey Decimal Classification: 306.73
Subject Heading: CHRISTIAN LIFE \ SEXUAL ABSTINENCE \ GOSPEL

Printed in the United States of America

Student Ministry Publishing
LifeWay Resources
One LifeWay Plaza
Nashville, TN 37234-0144

We believe that the Bible has God for its author; salvation for its end; and truth, without any mixture of error, for its matter and that all Scripture is totally true and trustworthy. To review LifeWay's doctrinal guideline, please visit www.lifeway.com/doctrinalguideline.

Unless otherwise noted, all Scripture quotations are taken from the Holman Christian Standard Bible®, copyright 1999, 2000, 2002, 2003 by Holman Bible Publishers. Used by permission.

CONTENTS

ABOUT THE AUTHOR

For more than 18 years, D.A. Horton has been teaching teenagers about biblical sexuality. He uses rap music as a tool to help educate the people of God on the precepts of Scripture as well as how to evangelize to the lost by presenting them with the gospel of Jesus Christ. D.A. currently serves as Pastor of Reach Fellowship, a church plant in North Long Beach, California, and as Chief Evangelist for the Urban Youth Workers Institute (UYWI). He holds a Master's in Christian Studies from Calvary Theological Seminary and is currently working on his Ph.D. in Applied Theology with a North American Missions emphasis at Southeastern Baptist Theological Seminary. He is also the author of *G.O.S.P.E.L., DNA: Foundations of the Faith*, and *Bound to Be Free: Escaping Performance to be Captured by Grace*. D.A. and his wife, Elicia, have two daughters, Izabelle and Lola, and a son, D.A. Jr. (aka Duce).

NOTE FROM THE AUTHOR

God is holy. He is absolutely removed from anything that is unholy or impure. God calls us to be holy as well, "You must be holy because I am holy" (Lev. 11:45b). This poses a problem for us—we are not like God. We are not holy. We are sinners, and our minds—our very ability to grasp God, has been tainted by sin to such a degree that we cannot please God (Rom. 8:8). This presents us with a seemingly unsolvable problem. God commands us to be holy and yet we are incapable of making ourselves holy. There is, however, good news. The gospel is the message of hope that informs people from every ethnicity, gender, and socioeconomic background of how we can be made holy when we embrace Jesus Christ as Lord and Savior.

The challenge for the remainder of life on this side of eternity for every Christian man is simplified as this: We are called to strive to be holy while simultaneously recognizing that we cannot be holy. The Bible calls us to a dependent striving. We make every effort to live a pure life while recognizing that the power to do so comes from outside of ourselves.

The focus of our study is not just to advocate abstinence from sexual activity until marriage, although this is an important factor. Rather, my prayer for the students who dig into this study is that they would gain a deeper understanding of the gospel and its implications in order to relate this message of hope to every area of their lives— their sexuality and beyond. The overall goal is to help shape a gospel-saturated view of life for every young person who engages this material. I have prayed over this study, asking God that He would help every young man and youth leader to mutually develop an ethic of purity instead of behavior modification, legalism, or a lifestyle that mirrors the world's pursuit of ungodliness.

ABOUT THIS STUDY

This study will work through seven key virtues essential to developing a rhythm of holiness each believer has been called to live out. Each virtue will be unpacked contrasting what our culture says about it with what God has said in His Word. My hope for you as you engage this study is that you will find the ammunition and support you need to walk in purity.

As we dig into God's Word and strive to accept its truth over and against the claims of our culture, we find a new foundation for what it means to be a man of God. We will not only cultivate seven virtues essential to holy living, but we will also challenge you to surround yourself with other men who are committed to the pursuit of Christlikeness.

My prayer for you as you progress through this study is that you will fall more in love with Jesus so that you might encourage other young men to do the same. Let's not be content with our culture's selfish view of love—let's strive for something more real, true, and beautiful. Let's max out the attributes of a holy life so that we might cultivate authentic love for Christ and authentic love for each other.

HOW TO USE

PRESS PLAY

Begin each session watching the video from D.A. Horton as a group. Read the opening passage of Scripture and take a few minutes to discuss guys' answers to the questions that follow.

DISCUSS

Start working through the following three sections: Culture, Christ, and Purity. The information in this portion of the study will guide guys to consider the cultural perspective to the topic of each session, and how we are to place our identity in Christ rather than let the culture define who we are and what we believe. Then, when we learn to root our identity in Christ, our lives will naturally reflect the personal holiness and purity Jesus calls us to.

The final section of Discuss is the Apply section. Here, you can conclude your time as a group by leading guys through a few more discussion questions and then guiding them to practically apply Scripture to their lives.

ON YOUR OWN

The final page of each session is designed for guys to complete on their own sometime over the course of the following week as they reflect on what they learned in the group time.

LEADER GUIDE

The Leader Guide at the end of this book contains specific helps and tips for you, as leaders. Every group is different, so we want you to be able to adapt this study for your specific group of guys. With that in mind, this section includes a variety of ideas, helps, and tips for you as you walk through this study with guys, pointing them to Christ and encouraging them to glorify God by pursuing a life of holiness.

MAXED
OUT

EPHESIANS 6:10-18

10 *Finally, be strengthened by the Lord and by His vast strength.* 11 *Put on the full armor of God so that you can stand against the tactics of the Devil.* 12 *For our battle is not against flesh and blood, but against the rulers, against the authorities, against the world powers of this darkness, against the spiritual forces of evil in the heavens.* 13 *This is why you must take up the full armor of God, so that you may be able to resist in the evil day, and having prepared everything, to take your stand.* 14 *Stand, therefore, with truth like a belt around your waist, righteousness like armor on your chest,* 15 *and your feet sandaled with readiness for the gospel of peace.* 16 *In every situation take the shield of faith, and with it you will be able to extinguish all the flaming arrows of the evil one.* 17 *Take the helmet of salvation, and the sword of the Spirit, which is God's word.* 18 *Pray at all times in the Spirit with every prayer and request, and stay alert in this with all perseverance and intercession for all the saints.*

We live in a culture where purity is rarely talked about. Our culture would rather talk about how to avoid the consequences of impurity (i.e. birth control and safe sex). No one talks about the sacredness of marriage and the concept of saving sex for marriage is almost laughable to many today. Our culture simply doesn't believe in purity.

Our churches, however, aren't always that much better as they often make the opposite mistake of fixating on not having sex as the one and only aspect of purity that matters. When we look at Scripture we see that while God calls us all to save sex for the covenant of marriage, there are many other equally important aspects of purity. Throughout this study we will discuss several of these key aspects. In so doing, our prayer is that you will develop a holistic understanding of purity as you seek to live for Christ and His kingdom.

▶ **PRESS PLAY**   Watch the Session 1 video as a group, then discuss the following questions.

DISCUSS

Consider the following questions as a group.

What are some of our culture's prevailing attitudes about purity? How does our culture define purity?

How does the Bible define purity? What are the key attributes of a pure life?

To be pure means to be morally clean—to be free from sin. It involves more than merely avoiding sinful decisions like having sex before marriage. In order to be pure or clean in God's sight, both our attitudes and our actions must be submitted completely to God (Ps. 24:3-4). Purity is a posture, a way of life that flows out of a relationship with God.

While none of us are pure (Rom. 3:9-11), we serve a God who offers to cleanse us from all our sins through faith in His Son (1 John 1:9; 1 Pet. 3:18). Once you trust Jesus as Lord of your life, the pursuit of purity begins. As we genuinely seek to know and follow Christ, He begins to open our eyes to what it means to be pure. In this study we will see that to pursue Christ is to grow in purity. This requires the development of seven key virtues: identity, redemption, love, humility, self-sacrifice, endurance, and biblical manhood.

DISCUSS

CULTURE

Have you ever played a video game that allowed you to create your own character and adjust his attributes? What attributes did you max out? Why?

What attributes does our culture encourage us to max out as young men if we want to be happy or successful?

Our culture is constantly telling young men that the key to happiness and success is to be athletic, popular, attractive, and influential. Our culture tells young men to look, act, and dress a certain way if they want to make it.

What are the attributes we must max out if we hope to live a life of holiness?

I have defined seven attributes or virtues that are essential to living a holy life. We will look at both the world and the Bible's definitions of the following virtues: identity, redemption, love, humility, self-sacrifice, endurance, and biblical manhood. We will look at how our culture defines each of these attributes and then contrast that with what the Bible has to say. According to Ephesians 2:1-3, we live in a broken world—a culture has been utterly wrecked by sin. If we look to the culture to help us understand love and purity, we will find ourselves wrecked as well. We must let the Scriptures which are inspired by God (2 Tim. 3:16-17) speak if we hope to find our bearings on love and purity.

In each session, the above virtues will be unpacked, taking into consideration the secular worldview, Scripture, and sometimes the legalism that has infiltrated the church. For example, in dealing with the area of sexual purity as it relates to abstinence from sex until marriage, I have witnessed some who held to a radical pursuit of purity prior to marriage and then they fell into adultery later on in marriage.

They never dealt with the pride in their hearts that took shape in the form of legalism. While these young people had a genuine heart to please God and save sex for marriage, their commitment to virginity took priority over their desire for God Himself. They were pursuing the appearance of purity when they should have been pursuing Jesus. As a result, they began to drift. Eventually they found themselves unable to live up to their own standards—they had made virginity into an idol. Sexual temptation can only be conquered by a holistic biblical understanding of purity.

CHRIST

The world is constantly telling us to seek pleasure at any cost. Our culture constantly barrages us with this philosophy through entertainment, social media, and peer pressure. Therefore, it is essential that we weigh the world's ways against the teaching of God's Word.

The world has a distorted view of purity. Simply put, it encourages you as a young man to do whatever you want, as long as you don't hurt anyone. This is a man-centered philosophy because it puts the individual at the center of the decision-making process. In other words, it puts you in charge and makes you ultimate. Let's see how Scripture presents us with a different picture than that of our culture:

Read Leviticus 11:44-45.

What does the word "holy" mean?

What do we mean when we say that God is holy? What does it look like for us to strive to be holy like God?

The word *holy* literally means "set apart." When used in reference to God, it describes His other-ness.

God is not like us (1 Sam. 2:2). He is all-knowing, all-powerful, and ever-present. He perfect in love, power, justice, and goodness.

In Leviticus 11:44-45, God is speaking to His covenant people. Because God is absolutely perfect, He cannot lower His standard of perfection. This is bad news for us. We are mandated by God to be absolutely holy, but we are not—we are broken, sinful, and rebellious. At the darkest reality of this truth is where we find the gospel. The gospel affirms the fact we're sinners who can never live out God's perfect standard. However, the gospel points us to Jesus Christ, who is fully God, and added full humanity to His nature in order to live out God's perfect standard in our place. When He suffered on the cross, He became a sponge and absorbed God's wrath in place of sinners like you and me. He surrendered his life, was buried in a grave, and rose three days later. The resurrection of Jesus Christ is evidence that the payment that He made for the sinners debt toward God was paid in full and accepted by God.

So now sinners of every ethnicity, gender, and socioeconomic background who come to Jesus and admit they are guilty and incapable of saving themselves can be forgiven! God declares sinners who embrace Jesus as not guilty because Jesus has endured their punishment. Jesus then clothes them in His perfect righteousness! So the perfect Father looks upon the sinner, who is now a Christian, and He sees the perfect life of Jesus covering them. They are a part of the people of God, and because of Jesus' perfect life, they are welcomed into an eternal relationship with God.

SANCTIFICATION

Read Romans 13:11-14.

Once you have trusted in Jesus for the forgiveness of your sins and are declared righteous in God's sight, what is next?

What did Paul mean when he said, "salvation is nearer than when we first believed" (v. 11)?

While Jesus saves us and seals us for eternity with Him in heaven the moment we believe (Eph. 1:13; 1 Pet. 1:3-5), there is another sense in which our salvation is not yet complete. The Bible speaks of salvation in past, present, and future terms—you have been saved (Eph. 2:8-9), you are being saved (2 Cor. 5:1-2), and you will be saved (Rom. 5:10). Paul challenged the church at Philippi to "work out [their] salvation with fear and trembling" (Phil. 2:12) because he understood that salvation is more than a one time event. Salvation is a process that begins the day we believe and continues the rest of our lives. Once we have been declared righteous through faith in Jesus, God calls us to begin the process of sanctification—the process of becoming what we are already declared to be. Sanctification is the process of gradually becoming more like Jesus. We will not be sanctified overnight or by our own power. It requires faith and effort. That is what this study is all about—how we, by God's grace and power, might strive to become more like Jesus by cultivating virtues He has given us as a means of growing.

According to verses 12-14, what does Paul challenge us to do?

How should our lives as Christians be distinct from the world with regard to purity? What does Paul challenge us to do in verse 14 to ensure that our lives are distinct?

Paul challenges us to put on Christ, to look to Him for strength and guidance in every area of life. Doing so contradicts the unholy lifestyle we used to live in before we met Jesus. To put on Christ, we must also put off who we were before we met Him. Colossians 3:10 tells us to put on the "new self"—the former life we used to live is gone because we are new creatures in Christ Jesus (2 Cor. 5:17). All of these passages point us as men to the reality that all of our sins (even our sexual sins) can be forgiven in Christ because of His perfect work! This truth should serve as the motivation to strive for holiness and purity in all areas of life, especially sexuality.

PURITY

One final passage that is important to this conversation is Ephesians 6:10-18. Here Paul reminds us that our struggle for purity is a spiritual battle. Because every Christian is engaged in a spiritual war, God has equipped us with the proper attire to walk in victory. The armor of God provides us with protection as we engage in battle. It is designed for warfare, not fashion. Striving for purity without using the tools God has given us—prayer, Scripture, accountability—is similar to thinking we are equipped for war simply because we own a few camouflage shirts.

Read Ephesians 6:10-20.

Who provides the equipment we need for spiritual battle (v. 11)? How can we make sure we are prepared to battle our impure desires?

THE ARMOR OF GOD

Spiritually speaking, we are not civilians. We are in God's army. In fact, Paul reminds us in 2 Timothy 2:4 that we, as good soldiers, should not get caught up in civilian affairs that distract us from our marching orders (the Great Commission). So, the way we protect ourselves while living on mission is by utilizing the battle gear and weaponry God has provided us.

As it relates to the armor of God, we must find balance between two extreme misconceptions; our effort alone provides us with spiritual victory and God's effort alone provides us with spiritual victory. In fact, the full armor of God reminds us spiritual victory is a cooperative effort. In Ephesians 6:11, Paul tells us to "put on the full armor of God," which means God supplies us with the armor, but we must put it on!

Make a list of the various pieces of equipment God provides for us to put on as we battle impurity. How is each essential to the fight?

God also provides us with clarity regarding what each piece of our armor does and how we are to use it. Ephesians 6:14-20 is one long run-on sentence in the Greek with two central verbs, "stand" and "take." Verses 14-16 describe how we "stand"; by putting on the belt of truth, breastplate of righteousness, having our feet shod with the gospel of peace, and using the shield of faith.

Let's take some time to work through these pieces of our armor:

BELT OF TRUTH
The belt of truth reminds us that a lifestyle of the Christian should be in harmony with the commands of Scripture. As it relates to the area of sexuality, Scripture teaches that God has given sex as a gift that is to be enjoyed between one man and one woman inside the covenant of marriage (1 Cor. 7:2-3; Heb. 13:4), and the means God has declared for the human race to reproduce (Gen. 1:28). Any sexual activity outside of the covenant of marriage is sin.

BREASTPLATE OF RIGHTEOUSNESS
The breastplate of righteousness speaks of the integrity of our spiritual walk with God, meaning our heart has been guarded by the righteousness of Christ and our lifestyle choices reflect this covering. It is a challenge for you to guard your heart by protecting it and not giving it to any woman besides your wife (Prov. 4:23-26).

FEET SHOD WITH THE GOSPEL OF PEACE
The gospel is the ground we stand on. Every step we take, we have both "peace with God" because of Jesus' finished work, and the "peace of God," knowing that if we're walking in obedience to His Word. We have no reason to fear being out of His will. We must trust God's leadership over every step we take. By doing this we'll never fear missing out on what the world is doing, and we will stay away from sexual sin (Prov. 3:5-6; Jer. 17:7-8).

SHIELD OF FAITH

The shield of faith gives us the ability to extinguish the attacks of the Enemy by trusting by faith all God has revealed in Scripture and applying the Bible's teaching to our lives. This involves taking every thought and filtering it through Scripture (2 Cor. 10:5) in order to determine if it is from God (if it's supported by Scripture) or the enemy of our soul, our flesh, or the world (if it contradicts Scripture). Remember, sexual sin starts in the mind first, so we must train ourselves to take our lustful thoughts to God's Word in order to fight off temptation to sin.

HELMET OF SALVATION

In verses 17-20, Paul describes what we're to "take" by commanding us to "take the helmet of salvation." Paul is telling us to guard our most vulnerable commodity, our mind, by resisting the massive blows (thoughts) the Enemy throws our way. Before we sin, we think about sinning. Our minds are the main battlefields of spiritual warfare!

SWORD OF THE SPIRIT

The sword of the Spirit is the Word of God, the Bible. Paul was not the only one who described the Word of God as a sword. The author of Hebrews said, "For the word of God is living and effective and sharper than any double-edged sword, penetrating as far as the separation of soul and spirit, joints and marrow. It is able to judge the ideas and thoughts of the heart" (Heb. 4:12). When it comes to the internal motivation of our actions, God's Word is powerful and fast acting. It exposes us from the inside out. Too often we lose the battles with the Enemy of our soul, the worldly system, and our flesh because we're not using our only offensive weapon!

I'm convinced many Christians do not walk in spiritual victory in purity over our sinful addictions (especially when it comes to sexual sin) and struggles because we're not using the weaponry God has given us. We're not leaning into the powerful truth of God's Word for the ammunition we need to overcome temptation.

Instead we turn to music, video games, friends, or we give in to temptation and sin. Not using the weaponry God has given us is like our military trying to fight ISIS with water guns! How foolish it would be for them to drop the weapons the government issued them to defeat the enemy and pick up plastic toys. If we use anything in our spiritual battle outside of the armor and weaponry God has given us, our Enemy will walk all over us. God is calling us to live lives of purity and He's given us all we need! Let's be the generation that introduces purity to our nation!

APPLY

What is the gospel? How does this message relate to your life?

Why is it crucial that we know and understand the gospel as we strive for purity?

List some areas of sin you struggle with. Then list the equipment God has provided you to battle against these sins (Eph. 6). What are you waiting for?

What desires do you need to cast off? What armor of God do you need to put on?

How might we support each other as brothers in Christ as we pursue purity?

READ

Read Matthew 4:1-11, taking special note of both the specific ways Satan sought to tempt Jesus, as well as how Jesus responded to each temptation.

REFLECT

In what specific ways have you been tempted to sin lately? What desires lie at the heart of these temptations?

How might you guard both your heart and your head against these temptations?

In Matthew 4:1-11, Jesus is tempted on three occasions and not once did He quote His favorite rapper, actor, or movie line instead, He quoted Scripture. That's using the sword! It is not enough, however, to merely quote Scripture as if that is all it takes to fight sin. Jesus didn't just quote verses from the Old Testament as a magic mantra to shut Satan up—He actively believed the truths and promises found in God's Word. He trusted God's promises to provide for, protect, and establish His kingdom. The same is true for us when we are tempted to give in to sin. Just like Adam and Eve, we are being tempted to forget God's promises and distrust His Word. We need to both know God's Word and ask God for the strength we need to trust in its promises.

RESPOND

Journal a prayer to God, acknowledging the areas of your life where you have been struggling to be holy as He is holy (Lev. 11:44-45). What promises of God will you remind yourself of as you fight temptation in this area? How will you remember the gospel as you seek to fight temptation this week?

IDENTITY

1 PETER 2:9-12

9 But you are a chosen race, a royal priesthood, a holy nation, a people for His possession, so that you may proclaim the praises of the One who called you out of darkness into His marvelous light. 10 Once you were not a people, but now you are God's people; you had not received mercy, but now you have received mercy.

11 Dear friends, I urge you as strangers and temporary residents to abstain from fleshly desires that war against you. 12 Conduct yourselves honorably among the Gentiles, so that in a case where they speak against you as those who do what is evil, they will, by observing your good works, glorify God on the day of visitation.

WELCOME

One of the key attributes we must max out if we hope to live a life of purity is that of identity. We must have a clear sense of who we are and what we are called to do. There are many counterfeit identities that our culture pitches to us—that the key to life is to be popular, successful, influential, or personally fulfilled. Our culture tells us that the formation of our identity is entirely up to us—we can be whoever we want to be and live however we want to live. While God has certainly made each of us unique and given us unique talents, gifts, and abilities, our ultimate identity is graciously given to us by our Heavenly Father. Today we will see how a relationship with Christ secures our identity as children of God and renews our purpose to live for His glory.

▶ PRESS PLAY

Watch the Session 2 video as a group, then discuss the following questions.

DISCUSS

What does our culture say about identity? Who we are?

What was Aleister Crowley's philosophy? How did D.A. summarize his philosophy?

In contrast to Aleister Crowley's philosophy, what does Scripture tell us about our identity—who we are?

What does it mean to be made in the image of God? How are we different from animals?

Being made "in the image of God" means that God has shared with us certain characteristics of Himself that He did not give to any other type of creation. To human beings alone God gave personalities that flourish in community, the ability to make rational decisions, and a soul that lives on throughout eternity. So we are unlike the animal kingdom, the plant kingdom, and nature itself. God designed us so that we might have a unique relationship with Him.

DISCUSS

CULTURE

If you were to ask students in your school or neighborhood who they are, what do you think they would say? How do most students today identify themselves?

If there is one dominant thought about identity today, it is this: everyone has the freedom to do whatever they want and be whoever they want. Now this philosophy isn't actually new. In Genesis 3 we find the serpent in the garden speaking to Eve, telling her God was preventing her from doing what she wanted by telling her not to eat from the tree of the knowledge of good and evil. The serpent essentially told Eve, "If you eat this fruit, you will be like God and He doesn't want that—God is holding out on you!"

THE ROOTS OF OUR REBELLION

Read Genesis 3:1-13.

What did the serpent say about God's Word (v. 1)? What tactics did Satan use to get Eve to doubt God's Word (vv. 4-5)?

What did Eve notice about the fruit of the tree of the knowledge of good and evil after listening to the serpent? What does this tell us about Satan?

Sin blinds us to the goodness and glory of God and deceives us into thinking that the world ought to revolve around us.

Eve took time to look at the fruit and saw it was beautiful—she believed it would provide her with nourishment and give her knowledge she didn't already possess. She ate the fruit and gave it to her husband, Adam, who was with her at the time. This is puzzling because I would like to think that if I was standing next to my wife and she was talking to snake, I would not stand there passively. I would do whatever was necessary to get us away from this talking snake, throwing things at it as we ran away. However, what we see here is that Adam and Eve's desire to be like God corrupted their minds such that they were unable to think clearly.

According to Romans 5:12, by disobeying God and eating the fruit, Adam and Eve invited sin and death into the world. When the parents of the entire human race fell into sin, we fell into sin as well.

Who were Adam and Eve made to be? What did God intend for them to do (see Gen. 1:26-28)?

How did Adam and Eve's sin affect their identity—how they viewed themselves (v. 7)?

How did their sin affect their relationship with God? How did it affect their relationship with each other?

God created us to know Him and live in an open relationship with Him, where both sin and Satan (the serpent) are not present. God provided humanity with an identity. We are His image bearers (Gen. 1:26-27) who He created to glorify Him by ruling over creation and cultivating it (Gen. 1:28).

When Adam sinned, our identity was distorted. We are still image bearers of God, however now that all of us have a knowledge of sin, we are addicted to it. As a result, we all have a distorted view of our own identity and we live in world filled with people who have a distorted view of their identities. Our identity as God's image bearers is constantly under attack. The world spends billions of dollars each year in marketing for various counterfeit identities. The result is that we are often insecure about the way we feel and view ourselves, and we waste our lives trying to fit in.

CHRIST

While we have all misplaced our identity by elevating ourselves over God, there is good news. God has done something to restore our identity and purpose. Those who have embraced Jesus Christ as Savior are a part of the people of God. Our identification is routed back to purity and holiness. It is kind of like a passport. When you apply for a passport as a United States citizen, you do so in order to be given the ability to enter and exit different countries, including your home country. While traveling abroad, the passport proves you are a citizen of another country. The passport allows you to visit another country for business or vacation while reminding you that your citizenship lies elsewhere. The gospel reroutes our identity, reminding us that we are created in God's image and the same gospel empowers us to live for Him.

Read 1 Peter 2:9-12.

Our passport has a photograph, essential information regarding our identity such as our name, birthday, Social Security number, height, and weight. All of these create a framework for who we are. If you are a Christian, however, your identity is firmly rooted in the finished work of Jesus Christ on the cross (see 1 Pet. 2:4-8).

Although we were born in sin (Ps. 51:5), when we embraced Jesus Christ as Savior our sins were washed away and His righteousness covered us. At that moment our destiny was rooted in what Jesus has done for us—not in our own abilities or strength.

First Peter 2:9-10 helps us reroute our identity away from self and to Christ, encouraging us to see that holy living is possible! When we focus on the fact that our identity is in Christ, it will keep us from dismissing, discounting, and becoming discontent with our calling to live on mission for the glory of God.

In verse 9, Peter sets up a contrast between two different types of people. Who are they and how are they different?

The phrase "but you" sets up a contrast between those who have embraced Christ and those who have rejected Him. We were all once a part of the group who rejected Christ, but those who truly believe heard the gospel and the Holy Spirit caused us to be made alive in Him (cf. Eph. 2:1-10; 2 Cor. 5:17-21).

Let's take a closer look at who Peter says we are in Christ in verses 9-10:

How are we a "chosen race"? What does this tell us about our identity?

God chose us to be part of His family! The fact that we are a "race" expresses that the body of Christ is one family—all believers are of the same kind, the same spiritual ethnicity. We must remember the "people of God" according to Revelation 5, 7, and 21 are made up of saints from every nation, tribe, and tongue. We are a multi-ethnic family. Our identity is not centered on our color or culture, but on the fact God "chose" us.

How are we a "royal priesthood"? How is this different from how the world encourages us to think of ourselves?

We are a "royal priesthood"—we are fit for a king because Christ is from a royal ancestry. This is humbling because we were born in sin and were outside of the family of God, but praise Jesus, His sacrifice allowed us to be adopted by God (Rom. 8:16).

In the Old Testament, the kings who ruled over God's people couldn't serve as priests. One example of what happened when a king of Israel over-stepped his boundaries is found in the story of Uzziah. According to 2 Chronicles 26:16-21, Uzziah tried to do the work of a priest and was judged by God and given leprosy. First Peter 2:4-6 says because of Christ we can offer up spiritual sacrifices—because of the work of our Great High Priest Jesus (Heb. 4), we have been granted direct access to God unlike the kings of the Old Testament.

How are we a "holy nation"?

Holiness is our national identification! We are no longer identified as citizens of the worldly system (Eph. 2:1-3). We are being sanctified; more increasingly separated and distinct from the world as God gives us the strength to walk in purity in all areas of life.

How are we a "people for His own possession"?

Sanctification refers to becoming what we are already declared to be—righteous through faith in Christ.

We were purchased with the blood of Christ and now the Lord owns us and cares for us every minute of every day. Paul tells us in Colossians 1:13-14, "He has delivered us from the domain of darkness and transferred us to the kingdom of His beloved Son, in whom we have redemption, the forgiveness of sins." What a blessing it is to be part of the people of God, who have holiness as our identification! All of this helps us understand we do not have to identify ourselves with the world and its ways.

The world does not desire holiness and they will try to distract us from remembering who we truly are. The world will tell us our identity is rooted not in Christ, but our sexuality. The world wants us confused about our gender, they want us to experiment sexually, and root our identity in our sexual orientation. We don't need to follow the world's voice. It is leading us away from our true identity. We need to listen to God's Word so that we might realize that our sexuality is not a right that we get to use however we want, but a gift to be engaged according to His will and for His glory.

What does Peter say about the purpose for which God has made us into "a royal priesthood, a holy nation, and a people for His possession" (v. 9)?

Peter now tells us the reason God did all of what we just discussed—"so that you may proclaim the praises of the One who called you out of darkness into

His marvelous light" (v. 9). God provided us with our new identify in order to send us out on a mission to make Him famous. The word "proclaim" reminds us that we are to continually talk about God's great work of salvation through Christ. Our lives are snapshots of God's work of salvation—we're His living #hashtag! He's worthy of trending! So we should then unashamedly proclaim His "praises"—His power to save sinners.

Through Christ, God has called us "out of darkness into His marvelous light." He's allowed us to push back the darkness of sin in our homes, communities, and schools by sharing the gospel.

PURITY

How should our identity in Christ shape our pursuit of purity?

Our calling is based on our identity. The world views their identity in their sexuality, career, achievements, relationships, and possessions. We are not to discount or cheapen our identity by thinking our value and worth is found in the temporary things the world places their identity in. Sexual sin leaves long-lasting consequences that encourage people to deal with their guilt by having more sexual encounters, abusing drugs, or diving deep into depression. Careers can be changed, jobs can be lost, possessions can be stolen, and relationships can break. All of this should encourage us to remind ourselves of our new identity in Christ. You belong to Him—He will never leave or forsake you (Heb. 13:5).

Look again at 1 Peter 2:10. How might the truth of this verse equip you to respond when the world does not accept you?

Those who have trusted in Christ have been given a secure identity in Him. Further, they have received mercy and as a result, all of their moral failures and insufficiences have not kept them from God. If you have trusted Christ, you are God's child—you no longer belong primarily to this world but to the One who created it.

How does sexual sin breed insecurities in us? How might knowing who we are in Christ help us overcome our insecurities?

The highway to sexual sin is paved with physical and emotional insecurities. If we don't get a lot of attention from girls we may feel like we're ugly and will never find love. This idea will cause us to explore the world of pornography under the false assumption that it will never reject us. In our insecurity we are drawn to pornography because we buy into the lie that it places our desire for sexual fulfillment on top of the priority list. But pornography is a destructive lie that will never satisfy us. It is a distortion of something that God created good (sex) that corrupts our hearts and objectifies people made in God's image. The world of pornography opens us up to a world of sexual scenery we were not meant to see until we're married and the images we view remain stuck in our brain and distort our view of sex. We can fight off entrance into the world of porn by looking at our passport of purity to remember our home is heaven. Holiness must be pursued so we can represent our God well in our homes, schools, and neighborhoods.

The struggle with insecurity is so real. It is what causes us to look in the mirror to evaluate our face, our clothes, and our shoes. If we struggle with affirmation regarding athletics, we will seek to excel athletically and gain the affirmation of people who we value. As Christians, we must strive to overcome our insecurities by not looking to other people for validation, but instead by looking back to God's Word in order to identify what holy living looks like.

How might remembering that we were made in the image of God help us regain a healthy view of ourselves?

Knowing that we were made in the image of God and that through Christ He has restored this image in us from the corruption sin has caused should radically change our perspective about ourselves and others. It should open our eyes to see that we don't have to be dominated by the impulses of our flesh—neither do our friends and neighbors. We can live in the confidence that Christ has saved us and called us to proclaim His praises and His power to push back the darkness around us.

APPLY

Read Romans 8:9-13.

What does this passage teach us about who we are and how God has equipped us to fight temptation?

God the Holy Spirit took up residence in our lives when we embraced Jesus as Savior. Romans 8:9-13 informs us that God the Holy Spirit supplies us with the strength that we need in the moment of temptation to say no to what our flesh wants. Through the power of the Holy Spirit, we possess the power to live with self-control. We do not have to fall into sexual sin, idolatry, or substance abuse.

After reminding his readers that they have the Holy Spirit, what does Paul tell them to do with their sinful desires in verse 13? What does that look like?

How does the gospel address the topic of your identity? How does this relate to your pursuit of purity?

Paul tells us that we are to "put to death" our sinful desires. In other words, we are to do whatever it takes to fight sin. We must learn to subject our fleshly desires to the Lordship of Jesus. We do this through times of prayer, reading Scripture, memorizing Scripture, meditating on Scripture's promises when we are tempted, and walking in self-control. We are to do all these things while constantly remembering the gospel—that we cannot fix ourselves, but that we have a Savior who is powerful where we are weak and who called us out of darkness and into His marvelous light.

What are some ways the world around you tries to shape the way you view your sexuality?

What are three practices you can put into place that will remind you that your identity is rooted in Christ?

READ

Read Hebrews 11:4-38 and make a list of the various people mentioned in these verses and how God used them for His mission and glory.

REFLECT

What did each of the people mentioned in these verses have in common?

How did their faith help them overcome their insecurities and weaknesses?

What insecurities and weaknesses with regard to sexual sin do you need to look to Christ for strength to overcome. Journal a prayer to God naming these weaknesses and asking Him for the strength to do whatever it takes to overcome them. Pray that He would help you live in the reality of who you are in Christ rather than the identity the world calls you to.

RESPOND

How might you remind yourself every day this week of who you are in Christ?

What is one radical action you need to take this week to put sin to death?

REDEMPTION

EPHESIANS 1:7-9

7 *We have redemption in Him through His blood, the forgiveness of our trespasses, according to the riches of His grace* 8 *that He lavished on us with all wisdom and understanding.* 9 *He made known to us the mystery of His will, according to His good pleasure that He planned in Him* 10 *for the administration of the days of fulfillment—to bring everything together in the Messiah, both things in heaven and things on earth in Him.*

PSALM 103:11-12

11 *For as high as the heavens are above the earth, so great is His faithful love toward those who fear Him.* 12 *As far as the east is from the west, so far has He removed our transgressions from us.*

ISAIAH 43:25

"It is I who sweep away your transgressions for My own sake and remember your sins no more."

The word "redemption" carries the idea of buying something back, such as an item from a pawn shop. According to Scripture, all people are slaves to sin and the debt we owe we cannot pay back on our own. When our first father Adam fell into sin (Gen. 3:1-7), he lost the purity he was created with and became separated from God. Along with sin comes a penalty and a price.

The penalty for sin is death and the price that comes with it is shed blood. God, desiring to have a relationship with us, with a heart of mercy, instituted a sacrificial system (Lev. 1–7). This system allowed the sins of those who desired to be in a relationship with God to have their sins symbolically covered by the shedding of the blood of an animal. This system reminds us of two important truths—our sin has grave consequences and we serve a good and merciful God.

All of this set up the coming of Jesus, the spotless Lamb of God (Heb. 7:26), who would be the one-time sacrifice for our sins (Heb. 10:1-25). Jesus wouldn't just cover our sins, but through His death He offers to completely wash away our sins once and for all. Through faith in Him, we can have our sin debt completely forgiven by God! Understanding the redemption God offers us in Christ is key to living a pure and holy life. The world around us disagrees with God's way of dealing with the debt of sin by telling us that forgiveness is limited and dependent rather than full and free.

▶ **PRESS PLAY** — Watch the Session 3 video as a group, then discuss the following questions.

DISCUSS

Apart from Christ, how is forgiveness always a gamble and not a guarantee?

How does Jesus make our forgiveness a guarantee?

Why is it important to remember that God forgives us according to the riches of His grace? How might remembering this help us grow in purity?

DISCUSS

How does our culture view forgiveness?

How is forgiveness, by our culture's definition, "a gamble"?

The world tells us we can make payments to offset our sin by doing good things. The world tells us we should give to the poor so we can have our consciences cleared for the wrongs we've done. In reality, forgiveness according to our culture is a gamble because it's not guaranteed. By this definition, we don't have to forgive those who have hurt us—we can hurt them back and make them feel the pain we've had to deal with. Culture says, "Forgive but don't forget."

Our culture wants us to think that forgiveness is optional—we can pick and choose who we give it to. The more a person hurts us, culture tells us, the less we have to forgive them. Our world is unforgiving: the more known an offense is, the longer the person who committed it is thrown under the bus. We see this when politicians or celebrities say something offensive or do something immoral—our culture will remind the world of their sin constantly through articles and memes.

This is a huge problem as social media provides us with new avenues to shame each other. How would you feel if every text you ever wrote, every picture you ever took, and every direct message you ever sent were published on the internet? How would people respond? Sadly, we live in a culture where this sort of thing happens and the results are often brutal as teens are bullied to the point that they consider committing suicide. If we hope to walk in purity, we need to acknowledge that we live in an utterly unforgiving world. As a result, we must look to the only One who can truly forgive our sins and empower us to walk in purity.

How do these cultural definitions of forgiveness compare with that of Scripture?

If we "forgive but don't forget," have we truly practiced forgiveness? Why or why not?

CHRIST

Read Ephesians 1:7-9.

According to Paul, how has God forgiven those who have trusted Christ?

The Bible tells us a completely different story than culture does. In Ephesians 1:7, Paul tells us that in Christ we have redemption and forgiveness for sin because Jesus shed His blood. According to Paul, we have continual forgiveness for our sins. We can never out-sin God's forgiveness. God will always forgive us for our sins when we ask Him because of what Jesus did for us on the cross.

How might remembering Christ's work of redemption help us overcome sexual sin?

Sexual sin has a way of making us feel unworthy to approach God and we buy into the lie we can deal with this guilt on our own, then try to ask for forgiveness once we've gone a few days, weeks, or months without falling into the same sexual sin again. This is not how God thinks at all! Let's work through the meaning of redemption to better understand how God views us after we've fallen into any type of sin, especially sexual sin.

Redemption refers to the act of paying off a debt for someone who can't pay it themselves.

We were unable to pay off the debt our sin racked up in the eyes of God, and the only payment God accepts is shed blood. This is where the gospel reminds us that Jesus shed His blood to make the payment God accepted to take away our sin debt by paying it in full. By dying on the cross for our sins, Jesus paid our debt.

Read Psalm 103:11-12 and Isaiah 43:25.

What do these verses tell us about how God treats those who look to Him for forgiveness?

Does God actually forget our sins when we look to Christ for forgiveness? Why or why not?

When we embrace Jesus as Savior we are granted full forgiveness for all of our sins. Forgiveness means to send something away forever, and when we become a Christian God sends our sin debt and guilt away forever. This does not, however, mean that God isn't aware of our past sins. God is perfect in knowledge. He knows us better than we know ourselves. He knows everything about us—past, present, and future (Ps. 139:1-6). When the Bible says that God will not remember our sins any more, it does not mean that He no longer remembers them, but rather that He actively chooses not to hold our sins against us. He is fully aware of our past failures and impurities. However, when we cry out to Him and trust in His Son for the forgiveness of our sins, He determines not to let our failures be the final word. His mercy triumphs over His judgment (Jas. 2:13).

Look at Isaiah 43:25 again. For whose sake does God promise not to remember our sins? Why is this good news?

God told Isaiah that He would forgive all who cried out to Him "for My own sake." In other words, God offers us forgiveness not merely because He loves us, but because He wants to display His mercy and grace to others. Forgiveness is a demonstration of God's glory. Just as God demonstrates His glory by offering us forgiveness, we are to demonstrate God's glory to others in the way we offer forgiveness to each other.

Read Colossians 3:12-13.

How can we "put on" the virtues listed in verse 12? Which of these do you most struggle to "put on"?

What does an unforgiving heart communicate about us?

The example we are to follow as we practice forgiveness in our relationships with others is the manner in which Jesus has forgiven us. We put on the virtues listed in verse 12 by looking to Jesus who was perfect in compassion, kindness, humility, and patience. Just as Christ has fully and freely forgiven us, we are to fully and freely forgive others. This does not mean that there won't be serious consequences for ours or others' sins. Some sins have serious consequences that cannot be avoided. We practice Christlike forgiveness when we choose not to continue holding the sins of others against them.

Look again at Ephesians 1:7. How is it good news that Jesus offers us redemption and forgiveness "according to His riches" not "out of His riches"?

What is the difference?

There is no limit to the forgiveness that God offers us in Christ. God is not stingy in handing out forgiveness to us. Remember the debt my parents forgave me of in the video? We cannot out-sin God's forgiveness.

Read Romans 6:1-14.

What is wrong with thinking that because we are fully, finally, and freely forgiven in Christ that we can live however we want?

Jesus worked very hard to set us free from sin and death. He did not take a wife. He did not have a home. Almost everywhere Jesus went, He was hounded by the Pharisees and Sadducees. He went into the desert and contended with Satan himself. In the end, Jesus allowed Rome to beat Him and crucify Him, and in that act, the very wrath of God Almighty was poured out onto His soul. He paid this price to set us free. How is it that after the Savior paid such a price, we would again pursue the things that He died to set us free from? This is essentially the point Paul makes in this passage. Jesus set us free by His death and resurrection. Because of this, sin's power over us is broken and we ought not go back to the sin that was destroying us.

If you think that because the forgiveness Christ offers is full and free that you can live however you want, you have missed the point. Even though we will always be forgiven for our sins, it shouldn't encourage us to go out and sin as much as we want. Doing so would completely contradict our new identity as those who are dead to sin. Romans 6:1-14 reminds us, we shouldn't sin to get more grace—sin is not our master, we don't have to obey our fleshly desires when we're tempted to sin.

How do we prevent sin from reigning in our mortal bodies?

Christ gives us the power to live obedient lives. We are a people under grace, and being under grace means we no longer need to fear the consequences of the law's just demands. The law says that the penalty for sin is death, but grace says that Christ paid that penalty for us. Because of this magnificent truth of God's love and mercy demonstrated to us in Christ, we ought to reject any attempt for sin to master us.

PURITY

Another blessed reality we must take time to consider about forgiveness is how God views us after we have fallen into sin, and the conviction we wrestle with when we realize we've sinned. This is why its important we work to know the difference between conviction and condemnation.

Read Galatians 6:1-2 and Romans 8:1.

What is the difference between conviction and condemnation?

Conviction takes place when God the Holy Spirit convicts us of the sins we've committed. The Spirit then moves us to confess our sin, turn away from it, and walk in community with other believers in order to practice repentance. Condemnation, on the other hand, urges us to run away from God. Condemnation tells us God no longer loves us, He won't forgive us because we've fallen into the same sin again, and that everyone around us will think less of us. All of these thoughts make us feel that we should run away from God instead of running toward Him. God the Holy Spirit will always convict us of our sin while leading us to confess and be restored spiritually (Gal. 6:1-2), while Satan will throw condemnation our way in order to get us to live in isolation, trapped by guilt and shame from our sexual sin.

How should we respond to the conviction of sin? What does Galatians 6:1-2 teach us about how we can help each other in that process?

This is a major struggle I wrestled with as a teenager while living with my parents. Between the ages of 13 and 15, I often lied to my parents by telling them I was going outside to play basketball, when really I was running the streets and committing various crimes. I often felt conviction about the lifestyle I was living, but I thought that if I confessed the way that I had been living to my parents that they would no longer accept me as their son. As my friends on the streets would entice me to spend more and more time out on the streets, my lies became more elaborate to the point when my mom and dad no longer let me go outside by myself.

This led to arguments between my dad and I. After one tense argument, I decided to run away. The first few days I was miserable—I wanted to go back, but I felt my mom and dad would no longer want me anymore. Little did I know they were calling the police, calling friends, and driving throughout my neighborhood looking for me the entire time. I ran away at least a dozen times and each time I was scared to come home, until the last time.

The very last time I ran away, I snuck back into the house after my mom and dad went to bed to get clean clothes. I noticed that my mom and dad had ordered pizza and actually left some on a plate for me, so naturally I ate it as quietly as possible. Then I walked into my room, grabbed extra clothes, and started to head to the front door. On the way out, I noticed several sticky notes on my desk. Each sticky note was dated with one of the days I had been out on the streets, and there was a handwritten note from my mom for each day. She constantly reminded me in each note that she and my dad loved me. They were praying for me, and they wanted me to come back home. As I read those notes, the condemnation that had grabbed hold of my heart evaporated and conviction began to sink in.

I realized how foolish I was to think that I wasn't good enough and didn't deserve to be welcomed back home. I was wrong! I came home and was embraced by my family. My parents assured me of their love for me, but explained how it broke their hearts when I ran away. I told them it was hard to receive their forgiveness because of all the wrong I had done by hurting them, but they reminded me they have hurt God more and He's always forgiven them. I never ran away from home again.

According to Romans 8:1, how does God see those who have trusted Christ for the forgiveness of their sins?

When we find ourselves caught up in sin, particularly sexual sin, we often begin to feel conviction, but we tend to sweep those thoughts away and wrongly assume God couldn't possibly love us because of how far we've fallen. As a result, we isolate ourselves from Scripture, church, our Christian friends, and others. It's during times like this when we must remember how God views those who are in Christ.

When Jesus was on the cross, He became a sponge and absorbed the cup of God's wrath that should have been poured out on us down to the last drop. Now, for us who are in Christ Jesus, we can live with confidence that God has no condemnation or wrath to pour out on us because Jesus took it all. We can come to Him when we feel conviction because we know we will be forgiven.

"Therefore, no condemnation exists for those who are in Christ Jesus."
—Romans 8:1

APPLY

How does the gospel address the topic of forgiveness?

How have you sought to forgive those who have hurt you deeply?

Is there anyone in your life you are withholding forgiveness from? How might you seek to reconcile with this person this week?

Who are some people you need to ask forgiveness from?

What sins do you need to confess and be forgiven by God for? How does confession lead to freedom from slavery to sexual sin?

READ

Read 2 Corinthians 7:5-13, taking note of the difference between godly sorrow and worldly grief. What motivates each? What does each lead to? Also list times you have responded to the sin in your life with worldly grief and examples of times you've responded with godly sorrow.

REFLECT

What is the difference between godly sorrow and worldly grief?

How can you avoid the pitfall of responding to the sin in your heart and life with worldly grief?

How can you strive to respond to the presence of sin in your life with godly sorrow?

RESPOND

Confess to God the times you've responded to sin with worldly grief—concerned about its consequences, but ultimately unrepentant about your actions. Ask God to give you true conviction—to make you grieve the damage your sin has done to your relationship with God and others.

LOVE

1 CORINTHIANS 13:1-7

1 *If I speak human or angelic languages but do not have love, I am a sounding gong or a clanging cymbal.* 2 *If I have the gift of prophecy and understand all mysteries and all knowledge, and if I have all faith so that I can move mountains but do not have love, I am nothing.* 3 *And if I donate all my goods to feed the poor, and if I give my body in order to boast but do not have love, I gain nothing.*

4 *Love is patient, love is kind. Love does not envy, is not boastful, is not conceited,* 5 *does not act improperly, is not selfish, is not provoked, and does not keep a record of wrongs.* 6 *Love finds no joy in unrighteousness but rejoices in the truth.* 7 *It bears all things, believes all things, hopes all things, endures all things.*

The concept of love has many different interpretations in our day. People use the word *love* very loosely. We talk about how we love our favorite sports teams or how we love Playstation 4 more than Xbox One. We use the word *love* to describe how we feel about our favorite foods, restaurants, hobbies, forms of entertainment, and artists.

Obviously the way we feel toward our family members when we use the word *love* means something different then when we're speaking about jobs, hobbies, or sports teams. If I say I love cheeseburgers, people should understand I do not have a romantic relationship with cheeseburgers. Context matters.

Because language can be confusing, we should be very careful to set up the proper context for even how we use the word *love* every day in our speech. Today we will develop a proper context for our understanding of love by looking at Scripture. In so doing, we will unpack God's view of love and discover how it is in direct conflict with our culture's definition of love.

▶ **PRESS PLAY**   Watch the Session 4 video as a group, then discuss the following questions.

DISCUSS

What is the difference between love and lust? What is dangerous about confusing the two?

How has God demonstrated His love for us? How should God's love for us shape the way we love one another?

What is wrong with the pick up line, "God told me that we are supposed to be together"?

DISCUSS

CULTURE

In our culture, people use the word *love* in a way God did not intend. People seem to show love for material things often with more care than they would other human beings. Some people have prized possessions like cell phones, cars, or gaming systems and they give these things more attention than they do the people who live in their house. Our understanding of love is so messed up that we willingly break off interpersonal relationships with people God has placed in our lives in favor of "hanging out" with people we don't actually know in online communities.

If all you knew about love was what you hear in popular music, movies, or TV, how would you define it?

In contrast, how does God's Word define love?

To refuse to give someone what they want because we think it is dangerous or unhelpful, by the world's definition of love, is hate.

The culture we live in says that as long as we let people have what they want, give them space to enjoy what they have, and never tell them their desires are wrong, then we love them. However, if we do the opposite by not giving them what they want or telling them they are wrong for wanting something, we are often charged with hate.

Deep down we know that the world's definition of love is ultimately destructive. For instance, if you had a friend or family member who was addicted to drugs, what would you do? You'd schedule an intervention. You'd get as many people who care about that person to confront him and surround him and plead with him to go to rehab and fight his addiction. To see a friend drowning under the weight of addiction and refuse to tell him that he is wrong is not love. We may not know the consequences of drug addiction first hand, but we all know the danger it poses to health and relationships. If you love someone, you speak up.

However, the person who is addicted to drugs often tells his family he hates them by trying to force him to choose between rehabilitation and the way he wants to live. So we see a conflict between definitions of love. Our culture wants us to believe that we can do whatever we want and not be held accountable for what we have done. For example, if a young man and woman give into sexual temptation and the girl becomes pregnant, our culture says, "That's not a problem. Just abort the baby." Or if someone visits the house of their friend and steals their video game, if they are busted, they expect to be able to just give the video game back and not face charges. We want to do what we want without accountability.

What is wrong with the world's definition of love?

In the video, D.A. talked about the pick up line, "God told me we are supposed to be together." What are we trying to accomplish with this line? Why is this ultimately unloving?

Faulty definitions of love do not only exist out in the world, they also exist in the church and particularly in youth group culture. Telling a girl that God told you the two of you are supposed to date is a prime example. When you say this, what are you doing? You are trying to get a girl to do what you want. It's manipulative and dishonest. It elevates your desires above her needs. If you tell a young woman this and then the relationship ends, what does that say about God? How might that make her feel? Christ calls us to higher view of love than that of the world. For God, love is never merely a feeling.

Why might you think God wants you to date that girl you like so much? It's ultimately because you have strong feelings toward her. God, however, demonstrates His love for us in action by sending Jesus to die on the cross for sinners like us (Rom. 5:8). In other words, Jesus was willing to sacrifice His well-being for the sake of serving us. We will spend the remainder of this session unpacking the amazing picture of true love Jesus painted for us on the cross.

CHRIST

The best way we can understand God's love is by looking at what He does, because God's view of love is always demonstrated in action.

Read 1 John 3:1.

What does John highlight about God's love for us?

How can we be sure that God loves us?

In 1 John 3:1, we see the apostle John telling us God's love for us motivated Him to perform the necessary actions for us to become His children. The actions I am referencing are those found in the gospel message.

Remember, the gospel reminds us we were born in sin (Ps. 51:5), slaves to sin (John 8:34), and separated from God because of our sinfulness. And yet Romans 5:8 tells us, "But God proves His own love for us in that while we were still sinners, Christ died for us!" This passage reminds us that while we were spiritually dead and slaves to sin, God still loved us and proved His love through action. God loved us when we were at our lowest. This truth should comfort us because now that we are in Jesus Christ, we can rest assured that He will love us for the long haul.

> Read 1 John 3:10-11 and John 13:34-35.

How should God's love for us shape and inform the way we love each other? How should it inform how we think about dating?

What does God intend to communicate to people outside the church through Christians' love for one another?

Our relationships with other followers of Christ are not a secondary matter. John says that if you do not love your brother, you are not a follower of Christ, and Jesus said that one of the primary ways people will be able to see that we are His disciples is through our love for one another in the church.

There is a great temptation today among young people to rush into romantic relationships. The Bible's teaching on love, however, reminds us not to let our emotions dictate our behaviors. Instead, we are to put the needs and desires of others ahead of our own and to desire for Christ to be glorified in us above all else. Before jumping into a romantic relationship, we should consider whether it will honor God. We should also consider our relationship with the person we would like to date—would dating her help or hinder her walk with God? Would it help or hinder your witness for Christ?

OUR LOVE IS A WITNESS FOR GOD

One reason it is important for believers to show the love of God to each other is in order to faithfully witness to the non-believing world. Not everyone comes from a loving family. Although God created us to live in community with other humans, we naturally have a desire to be accepted and loved by people. When people do not have a sense of love, safety, and community, they will seek these things outside the home and the church. This is why we sometimes turn to sports or teammates for acceptance. Although there is nothing inherently bad about finding love and acceptance among teammates, it can become dangerous when we base our love for each other on performance, which often happens in sports.

Other times, young men search for love with certain cliques or gangs. The love young men experience in gangs is conditional; it requires participating in sinful and even illegal activities. We should all be convicted to embrace and show God's love to such people. When nonbelievers are searching for love and look at our interpersonal relationships as brothers in Christ, they see the love of God put on display, love that is based not on performance but on loyalty. Then they will be more open to hear the gospel having seen the implications lived out in front of them.

PURITY

Read 1 John 3:16.

Understanding how Christ's love was demonstrated through action should carry over to the way that we treat young ladies. We should see them as our sisters in Christ. When it comes to the way we engage with girls, we have to remember 1 John 3:16 which says, "This is how we have come to know love: He laid down His life for us." Remember, Jesus showed His love for us by dying for us. John reminds us that we should be willing to do the same for other believers. We can apply this to relationships and friendships with girls by respecting, honoring, and serving them rather than using them.

What are some practical ways we might "lay down our lives" for each other? What might this look like in your relationships with girls?

God's love does not lead us into manipulating girls into relationships, acting on our lustful impulses for sexual gratification, or even being overly flirtatious and trying to get as many girls to like us as possible. God's love sets the boundaries for our friendships with girls to the point that we should seek to protect them like sisters, not just from nonbelievers, but often even our own selves.

To put it plainly, "laying down your life" in the context of your relationships with girls might mean refusing to date or even flirt with them, knowing that doing so would not point them to Christ.

I wish I had received the advice I am giving you when I was a teenager. I had girlfriends who were in the youth group with me, in addition to girlfriends who were not believers. Each and every one of those relationships did not end well. On many occasions, the girls cheated on me and over the course of time, I grew more insecure of myself. The way I would deal with my insecurity was by flirting with lots of girls. I would make them laugh, hoping they would like me. I would never make a formal commitment to them; however, I would spend hours on the phone with them speaking about life and future plans and making emotional investments in relationships that weren't labeled and lacked any firm commitment.

Over the course of time the girls would grow frustrated with me because I would never commit to our relationship or would eventually start ignoring them altogether. By my actions I was leading them to believe that we were in an exclusive relationship, but my intentions were selfish. I wanted to look cool and feel wanted and desired. I was not looking out for the hearts or interests of my sisters in Christ. My actions were neither kind nor Christlike.

I wish someone would have challenged me with the truth of 1 John 3:16. I should have put to death my own insecurities that led me to flirt and ultimately use and manipulate these girls. This would have allowed me to protect their hearts from confusion. Instead I was selfish and, as a result, may have scarred their future relationships. Perhaps you are on the other side of things, perhaps in your relationships with girls you have been on the receiving end of hurt and manipulation. Whichever side you find yourself on, the gospel calls us to remember His love for us and let that love guide and shape our love for others. Consider the impact of Christ's sacrifice for us, which gives us hope and confidence. It reminds us that we are loved eternally by the God who made us. It also frees us from holding the sins of others against them as our Heavenly Father chose not to continue holding our sins against us, but sent His Son to take our punishment and restore us to a right relationship with Him (1 Pet. 3:18).

Read 1 Corinthians 7:1-7.

How does Paul define love? Make a list.

How does Paul's definition of love compare to our culture's definition which we discussed at the beginning of this session?

When I was 20 and Elicia, who is now my wife, and I had been talking for about six months, I asked her mom and dad to have a private meeting with me. Sitting around the dinner table, I told them that I had completed a time of fasting, praying, and reading through 1 Corinthians 13:4–8. I expressed to them that I was convicted if I was not God's best for the Elicia, because I loved her with the love of God, I would remove myself from the relationship. I did not want to be a distraction in her pursuit of Jesus and I desired God's best for her life, even if that meant God had someone else for her.

Elicia's parents were touched that I would strive to make sure her heart was protected. I then asked for their permission to give her a promise ring the next week on Christmas Day. I told them my intention with the promise ring was to enter a formal relationship with her that would lead to an engagement and then marriage, and they gave me their blessing. I told them I would revisit this conversation with them privately when I was ready to propose. Nine months later I met with her parents again. It was then that I asked for permission to marry their daughter. To God's glory, Elicia and I have been married for nearly 14 years now.

I share this with you so that you will learn from the mistakes I made before I arrived at a clear biblical definition of love. Sadly, prior to my relationship with Elicia, I had given into the world's definition of love and pursued girls only for my own emotional, physical, and sexual gratification. I brought a lot of unnecessary baggage into my relationship with Elicia all because I had bought into the culture's definition of love.

How would your relationships with girls change if you viewed them as sisters in Christ rather than potential girlfriends?

Seeing the girls in your life primarily as sisters in Christ allows you to point them to Christ and to cultivate a faithful gospel witness to the non-believing world. When we show the love of God to our brothers and sisters, we will be willing to work through any disagreements, arguments, or even breakups that we may have. We will walk in forgiveness towards each other. We will seek to protect the hearts of those in the body of Christ, allowing them to enter into marriage with less emotional baggage and insecurities than I did.

God's love for us is steady and unwavering. God does not love us more when we obey, and He does not love us less when we disobey. His love for us is steady and faithful. This is the flavor of the love we should show those in the body of Christ. God's love is not based on our performance, rather it is demonstrated toward us on a daily basis. So let us love one another as God has first loved us (1 John 4:7-8), so that the world would put their trust in our Savior Jesus, receive His love, and freely give it as well.

Seeing the girls in your life primarily as sisters in Christ will help you to put first things first.

APPLICATION

In what areas of your life are you most tempted to give into our culture's thinking with regard to love and relationships?

What does the gospel tell us about God? About ourselves? About everyone else?

The gospel is the only sure antidote to selfish living as it transforms our view of God, ourselves, and our neighbors. If left to ourselves, we will continue to see the people around us as mere objects that exist for our own personal pleasure. In so doing, we will damage both our own personal purity and the purity of others. The gospel, however, reminds us that God is holy. We are to pursue holiness as His representatives. The gospel also reminds us that we are sinners in need of God's grace, reminding us of our tendency to fall back into selfish action. The gospel tells us that the people around us are created in God's image and are therefore deserving of the utmost respect. If our relationships are a mess, it might be a sign that we either haven't believed or perhaps we have not thought deeply enough about the gospel.

Read John 13:34-35 again. If people were to judge your character based solely on your relationships with the people closest to you, what would they conclude?

How will the way you interact with girls change based on today's session?

How will you put the needs of others ahead of your own needs this week? How might you discipline yourself to do this on a regular basis?

READ

Read Ephesians 5:22-33 taking note of how Paul describes marriage and what he expects of husbands and wives in a Christ-centered relationship. Take note of how God's vision for love and marriage is different from that of our culture.

REFLECT

What does this passage teach you about marriage? About love?

What does God expect of husbands? How are they to love and lead their wives?

Are you prepared for the kind of commitment that is demanded of Christian husbands in Ephesians 5? Jot down some areas where you need to grow:

RESPOND

Have you given into our culture's definition of love? Have you fallen prey to a selfish view of love thinking that it is all about getting what you want? Take some time to evaluate your view of love. Consider the times when you have operated or made decisions based on a faulty view. Ask God for the strength necessary to begin striving toward a more Christlike view. Ask Him to help you take steps this week to begin living out the gospel by serving the people around you and putting their needs ahead of your own.

HUMILITY

ISAIAH 66:1-2

1 *This is what the LORD says:*

Heaven is My throne,
and earth is My footstool.
What house could you possibly build for Me?
And what place could be My home?
2 *My hand made all these things,*
and so they all came into being.
This is the LORD's declaration.
I will look favorably on this kind of person:
one who is humble, submissive in spirit,
and trembles at My word.

WELCOME

Pride is a virtue in our culture. We hear boastful speech coming out of the mouths of people like water from a fire hydrant on a regular basis at school. Students regularly brag about what they did over the weekend, achievements they have accomplished in sports or in extracurricular clubs, and they even brag about their relationship drama. I have noticed that people love to talk about themselves. If you just sit there and listen, they will keep on boasting.

It's not just students in school; pride is in every sphere of influence in our culture. Pride is evident in movies as the "heroes" often refuse to listen to the counsel of others and rely completely on themselves. Pride is arguably most evident in the music industry as singers constantly produce songs about money, accomplishments, and sexual relationships. In sports, superstar athletes have multimillion dollar contracts, yet treat fans in a rude manner, boast in interviews, and even throw their teammates and coaches under the bus when convenient. Jesus, however, turns our culture's view of pride on its head and calls us to stop trying to prove how great we are. Jesus calls us to open our eyes to how desperately we need Him. It is only when we recognize our need that we will be in a position to serve and point others to Christ.

▶ PRESS PLAY

Watch the Session 5 video as a group, then discuss the following questions.

DISCUSS

How are Jesus' values different than those of our culture with regard to pride?

D.A. said we are fixers. How does our sinful nature distort our God-given desire to fix, build, and create?

How can we do these things—fix, build, and create—in a manner that glorifies God?

Why is it important that we learn to declare spiritual bankruptcy?

CULTURE

Does our culture tend to view pride as a virtue to be pursued, or as a vice to be avoided? What are some examples?

Are guys affected differently by pride than girls? How so?

Our sinful hearts turn our competitive spirit into a destructive force that keeps us from God and hurts our neighbors.

Men love to compete. There is a God-given longing inside most men to win; however, when that longing is coupled with a sinful heart, things get out of hand. We dedicate space on our walls and in our rooms for the collection of awards we have gathered throughout life. These things are not necessarily wrong, but when we place our identity in them, these things show who we truly are. If all we ever talk about is ourselves and our accomplishments, then we are no better than the world. If left unchecked, our drive to be excellent can turn into a desire to smash our competition and prove how much better we are than other people.

God created us to be conquerors—to subdue the earth (Gen. 1:28); however, He never intended us to do so as a means of proving our own greatness. God created us for His glory (Isa. 43:7). As young Christian men, we must be very careful to guard our hearts from the sin of pride. We must learn to leverage the abilities, gifts, and talents God has given us for his glory and not ours. This does not mean that we have to quit sports, stop being great students, or stop playing video games. Rather, we should seek to do everything for God's glory and leverage the attention we do receive to give Him praise and point people to Christ.

WE ARE FIXERS THAT DON'T LIKE FAILURE

In the conversations I've had with men of all ages, one common theme I see is that we all like to fix things. If you are a basketball player and you see your friend shooting poorly, you will give him tips about technique and maybe even offer to shoot with him after practice. Or if you are into video games, what happens when you see someone failing to complete a level? You will offer to take the controller out of their hands and complete it for them. As a man, when you see someone or something failing in an area that you are passionate about, there is a high probability that you want to help them fix the problem they are having.

While God has wired us this way, our desire to fix things can actually keep us from Him. Our desire to be fixers can puff us up with pride and blind us to the reality that we need God to fix us.

How do you respond when you see someone failing at something that you are good at or passionate about?

Do you see yourself as a "fixer"? Why or why not?

The opposite of pride is humility, and I believe this is the heart posture God wants all of us to adopt no matter how gifted we are. Yet, as fixers, we often think that we can fix ourselves, so we refuse to turn to God for help. The world is actually coaching you to think you don't need God or anyone else—you can fix yourself. Have you ever heard the saying, "God helps those who help themselves"? Guess what? You won't find this phrase in the Bible. In fact, Scripture says the complete opposite.

CHRIST

Read Matthew 5:1-3.

Matthew 5–7 is known as the Sermon on the Mount and it contains the longest single stretch of Jesus' teaching found in the Gospels. Here Jesus continues preaching the good news of the kingdom of God, which He is bringing from heaven to earth (Matt. 6:9). In this sermon, Jesus constantly turns the values and priorities of the world on their head. One of the first values Jesus turns on its head is our culture's assumptions about pride.

Who was the Sermon on the Mount addressed to (vv. 1-2)?

How does Jesus open the Sermon on the Mount (v. 3)? Does this surprise you?

Matthew 5 begins by telling us that Jesus saw large crowds of people following Him, and as a result, He went up on a mountain—presumably to put some space between Himself and the overwhelming crowd. When He did so, His disciples came to Him.

In other words, the Sermon on the Mount is primarily addressed to the disciples—those who had chosen to follow Him.

As Jesus taught, the crowds He had left behind would have found Him on the mountain and listened in. Given that Jesus would challenge His disciples to see themselves as salt and light (Matt. 5:13-16), it seems that Jesus singled out His disciples in this sermon in order to challenge them to impact the crowds by their words, actions, and values.

The first value Jesus identifies as essential to being His disciple is humility (Matt. 5:3). Jesus says, "The poor in spirit are blessed, for the kingdom of heaven is theirs." The phrase "poor in spirit" really means to declare spiritual bankruptcy. Now in the world of money, bankruptcy is when a person willingly admits that he or she cannot pay the debt they owe. The amount they owe exceeds their income such that paying off the debt is impossible. The person filing for bankruptcy will then hire a lawyer who will plead the case at court in hopes that the judge will agree that he or she cannot pay back the debt and declare bankruptcy. The person filing bankruptcy could be given a discharge which tells all of their creditors their debt has been forgiven and they no longer owe them anything.

What keeps us from seeing ourselves as spiritually bankrupt?

Why is seeing ourselves as spiritually bankrupt essential to following Jesus? How does this view promote spiritual growth?

How does the gospel help us maintain an accurate view of ourselves?

According to Jesus, unless you admit that your sin debt is too great for you to pay off and allow Jesus' blood to wipe away your sin, you will not be a part of the kingdom of heaven. The gospel reminds us that Jesus paid our debt on the cross, and His resurrection from the grave was God's way of saying the payment Jesus made on our behalf was accepted—we are now discharged from all guilt and punishment!

Pride prevents us from declaring spiritual bankruptcy. Trying to find our own way out of spiritual debt prevents us from declaring spiritual bankruptcy. Humility leads us to the reality that we need Jesus to pay off our debt. The world rejects this philosophy because they love pride; however, Christians should embrace humility so that we can be accepted by God.

GAINING GOD'S ATTENTION

Pride's appetite is increased by the attention of others. When people brag, they talk loud so that others can hear them. Their goal is to make themselves seem great in the eyes of others—the more people are watching and paying attention to them, the more their pride is fed. However, consider this: if you knew how to gain God's attention, would you do what God requires to get Him to pay attention to you? If so, let's look at Isaiah 66:1-2.

Read Isaiah 66:1-2.

Before we get into what this passage says about how we might gain God's attention, we should note that this passage reminds us of both God's position and our own. God reminds us that heaven is His throne and earth is His footstool (v. 1).

On whom does the Lord look favorably (v. 2)? What does that tell us about how God wants us to live as young men?

In verse 2, Isaiah quotes God saying, "I will look favorably on this kind of person: one who is humble, submissive in spirit, and trembles at My word." This verse is set up by verse 1 where God declares He is the Creator of all things. Heaven is His throne and earth is His footstool. God essentially asked Israel, "What house can you build that could contain My greatness?" Well, there isn't a house large enough because heaven can't contain God's matchless glory! Picture it this way, you and I live in some type of dwelling (e.g. apartment, duplex, house, etc.) and we don't fill all the space where we live because we're limited by our physical bodies. God says He lives in eternity because of how great He is! In other words, God is in a position of power, authority, and knowledge, whereas we are in a position of weakness and need.

What do these verses teach us about God? Why is it important to remember where God is?

What is the implied answer to the questions God poses in verse 1? What does that tell us about ourselves?

God then says everything that has been created has been created by Him. Think about the beautiful landscapes of the world, the mountains, the ocean, sunsets, palm trees, the gorgeous starlit skies at night—everything in creation is the product of our good and glorious God. In addition, He has equipped human beings with talents and abilities to create things as well, in order to reflect His creative genius. Think of all the wonderful things human beings have created from city skylines to manicured front lawns, to different vehicles for transportation, and all the technological advances we have. God says no matter how beautiful His creation or the things that human beings have created appear to be, those things do not capture His attention when He sees someone who is living in humility.

How does exercising humility require strength? Where can we find the strength we need to walk humbly before God?

That's the secret: living in humility attracts the attention of God. Not only does it attract His attention, He says He looks favorably at this kind of person. That means God looks at us solely with the intention to bless us because of our humble and submissive spirit. The word *humble* in this passage means to be weak and needy. This is the opposite of what the world says, because they believe we need to be strong and never confess we have a need. Remember, worldly thinking prevents people from declaring spiritual bankruptcy and receiving salvation.

Notice I said, "the person who is *strong enough* to admit they are broken." It does not take much strength to act like we have it all together because when we are alone then we can let our guard down and be the real us. However, it takes real strength to walk as the same person we are privately in public, constantly showing we do not have it all together and that we need help. We have all been broken by sin and had desires to fix our brokenness. This is the reality of the gospel message. Our brokenness becomes something that is beautiful in the hands of God because He makes us whole again when we embrace Jesus as our Savior and King.

Psalm 34:15 says, "The eyes of the LORD are on the righteous, and His ears are open to their cry for help." This Scripture reinforces what Isaiah said. God is looking upon those who are righteous. The gospel reminds us that when Jesus saves us, He washes us from our sins and clothes us in His righteousness. So from the moment that we become a Christian, God sees us as being righteous, pays attention to us, and is ready and willing to help us when we cry out for His help. This is what humility looks like, constantly making God aware of our need for Him!

> God looks with favor on the person who is submissive in spirit—the person who is strong enough to admit they are broken receives the favor of God.

PURITY

ADMITTING WE ARE BROKEN

The world wants us to think that men cannot show weakness in the form of admitting we need help. Remember, the world says we are fixers. We should not be broken, yet the Bible actually encourages us to openly admit our brokenness so that He can fix us! The word "broken" in Psalm 34:18 means that a person who has a broken heart has been completely crushed. It's similar to a bag of ice that we buy from the local grocery store or gas station when we go to a barbecue. Before we can use it, we have to toss it on the ground a few times to break up the ice because when a bag of ice sits in a freezer for a long time, it clumps up and freezes together.

How can we be more aware of brokenness and less filled with pride?

In a similar way, when we give into the rhythm of the world and we build ourselves up to begin walking in pride, we get clumpy and we need to be broken to be used by God. The trials of life, confessing our sin, and walking in accountability with other brothers in the Lord are all methods God uses to break the pride in our hearts so that we will cry out to Him. When we cry out, our God is near and will help us. It should comfort us to know that God the Holy Spirit, from the moment we are saved throughout all of eternity, takes up residence in our hearts (Rom. 8:9-13; Eph. 1:13-14). This should comfort us because it reminds us that God is not only near us, the Holy Spirit lives inside of us and gives us the strength to endure through times when our hearts are broken.

GIVING GOD AFFECTION, ONCE WE HAVE HIS ATTENTION

Now that we have seen that God's attention is on those walking in humility, let's discuss how we can live in humility while we have His attention. Isaiah says God is focused on the person who trembles at His Word. God is specifically attentive to the person who not only reads the Scriptures, but also studies it in order to live out His teaching. So basically, when we have God's attention, let's show Him that we love Him by walking in humility like the Scriptures command.

> Read Philippians 4:6 and James 1:2-5.

To the person who is humble, God gives grace, which means favors that he or she did not work for or earn. According to these verses, God is regularly trying to tilt us to drop our pride, admit we are broken, and let Him fix us with His grace.

Another means of fighting pride and striving for humility is prayer. There is no greater display of pride than when we do not pray. On the other hand, there is no greater display of humility than when we pray to God. When we pray, we are admitting that we are weak, broken, and are in need God's help. The key is praying without doubting. Philippians 4:6 says, "Don't worry about anything, but in everything, through prayer and petition with thanksgiving, let your requests be made known to God." This passage is a great reminder why we as Christian young men should not stress over the issues we face in life. We have a relationship with the Creator and Sustainer of the universe who can fix any issues that we have.

Secondly, because we live in a broken world, we will face trials. When this takes place, we should remember to have an attitude that reflects James 1:2-5. Then, we should take our situation to God in prayer and couple our requests with words of thanksgiving, showing that we trust God will work all things out for His glory and our good (Rom. 8:28). In doing this, we are walking in obedience to His command for us to remain humble.

Our world needs more young men love Jesus and demonstrate their love for God by walking in humility. Use everything God has given you in this life—abilities, gifts, life situations, and the whole of your life story—for His glory by walking in humility and challenging those who are watching you to do the same. Starve your pride by not focusing on the attention of your peers and random onlookers at school; rather, focus on having an audience of one: God.

APPLICATION

How does the gospel address the sin of pride?

How has pride manifested itself in your life lately? How will you combat your pride with the truth of the gospel?

Identify two steps you will take this week to begin walking in humility.

How does biblical humility connect to your sexual purity?

READ

Read Philippians 2:1-11, taking note of how Jesus demonstrated true humility throughout His earthly ministry and in His death.

REFLECT

How does Jesus exhibit the values and virtues Paul mentions in verse 1?

In what ways is your attitude different from that of Jesus (vv. 5-8)? How might you strive to adopt the attitude of Jesus this week?

What was the result of Jesus' humility (vv. 9-11)? How does this give you hope?

RESPOND

Thank God for sending His Son to take on human flesh and dwell among us. Thank Him for His astounding act of humility in living the life we could not live and dying the death we deserve. Pray that He would strengthen you to live humbly for His glory. Confess to Him your pride in desiring the praise of people, particularly the attention and affection of girls. Ask Him to give you the attitude of Christ with regard to purity and that you would put the needs of others ahead of your own selfish appetites.

SELF-SACRIFICE

ROMANS 13:11-14

11 *Besides this, knowing the time, it is already the hour for you to wake up from sleep, for now our salvation is nearer than when we first believed.* 12 *The night is nearly over, and the daylight is near, so let us discard the deeds of darkness and put on the armor of light.* 13 *Let us walk with decency, as in the daylight: not in carousing and drunkenness; not in sexual impurity and promiscuity; not in quarreling and jealousy.* 14 *But put on the Lord Jesus Christ, and make no plans to satisfy the fleshly desires.*

WELCOME

The characteristic of self-control is often offensive to our culture because it says we should control our passions rather than our passions controlling us. Our ease of access to the internet and social media makes holy living very challenging for students today, particularly for young men. As men we have been wired by God to have a sexual drive, but this God-given passion has been distorted by our sin nature such that we think of sex primarily in terms of personal fulfillment rather than a gift from God to be guarded and exercised according to His design.

The culture around us does not encourage self-control. Our culture responds to the sexual urges of young men with a multitude of outlets to exercise them such as pornography, dating apps, and hookups. While we might think that all these outlets would bring us freedom and satisfaction, they actually do the opposite—they enslave us. The more we give in to our passions, the more they control us and drive our decision making process. Think about it, with our cell phones, iPads, laptops, and personal computers, the internet brings the world of sin to the palm of our hands with the click of a button. In today's session, we will seek to uncover the lies our culture tells us about our desires and uncover Scripture's teaching not only on self-control, but also on self-sacrifice. True satisfaction can only be found when we let go of our selfish desires and live for something bigger than ourselves, namely the glory of God and the kingdom of Christ.

▶ PRESS PLAY
Watch the Session 6 video as a group, then discuss the following questions.

DISCUSS

What is wrong with letting your passions and desires drive you? How does the Enemy use our desires to hinder our pursuit of purity?

D.A. challenged us to wake up, wipe our eyes, and walk right. Why are each of these essential to the pursuit of purity?

What is God calling you to sacrifice for the sake of living for the glory of God?

CULTURE

Do you sometimes find yourself mindlessly scrolling through your Facebook timeline, Twitter, or Instagram feed? Why do we do this?

How do you think social media (Twitter, Instagram, Facebook, Snapchat, etc.) affects us?

If we are wrestling with loneliness, the culture tells us to build online relationships through social media. Through Facebook, Snapchat, Twitter, and Instagram we are able to gain followers, follow people back, and share our life with them on a public platform. This causes us to buy into the lie that we can create our own community. If someone says something that offends us, all we have to do is unfollow, unfriend, or block them. If somebody doesn't follow us after we have followed them, we get offended and we unfollow them. We read our insecurities into people's posts and assume they are talking about us when they aren't. We spend hours lurking on social media, looking at people's pictures, wondering why we weren't in them, and developing a fear of missing out.

All of this drama can be avoided if we just have conversations with people and learn to work through conflict by resolving it biblically. This is what self-sacrifice looks like. If we hope to see through the lies of our culture with regard to our desires, we must build relationships that are meaningful. More than ever, we need to discipline ourselves to build relationships with people in person; otherwise, we will continue to build a facade—a fake identity that doesn't really exist.

The culture also tempts us to engage with more and more information when we're bored. Engaging in this information may or may not be helping us grow. We may find ourselves wasting hours and hours scrolling and watching, clicking, laughing, liking, and commenting. We do all of this because we are bored or perhaps because we do not feel we are being entertained enough. We will push back work that needs to be done at home or for school in order to find our entertainment online.

What is our culture's attitude about our desires? Where does this attitude come from?

The world wants our passions to dictate our decision-making process. The world wants us to fear that we are missing out if we do not give in to our passions. When we look at God's design for life, we will quickly see that the culture is wrong, and we are wrong if we follow its cues for living. When you think about it, our flesh is never satisfied. Let me explain. The reason the world keeps throwing so much information at you nonstop is to keep you from practicing self-control.

The Enemy who runs the worldly system (Eph. 2:1-3) knows Christians have the Holy Spirit. He knows we have the power to say no to temptation, so Satan distracts us with an endless sea of outlets to exercise our passions. He knows that our flesh is never fully satisfied, especially after we sin. Take a moment to think about your own life. One sexual encounter does not satisfy you for a lifetime. One look at pornography, one experience with masturbation, or one make-out session is never enough. Giving into temptation doesn't fill our longings, but fuels our discontent and distracts us from our mission of living for the glory of God and the kingdom of Christ.

It works the same way with pride, one word of praise from one person does not give us the confidence to deal with a life of rejection afterward. One glance at social media does not satisfy you to the point where you never have to look at it again. For every text message that we send, we anticipate to receive a text message back, and the cycle continues on and on and on. The Enemy of our soul knows our flesh is never satisfied and he wants us to waste our lives chasing our passion for pleasure. This is why the battle to live out the virtue of self-sacrifice, which is submitting ourselves, our whole selves to God, is a lifelong struggle.

CHRIST

In contrast to our culture, what does Scripture say about how we should handle our passions and desires?

What value is there in controlling and even sacrificing our desires?

In contrast to our culture, Scripture indicates that self-sacrifice is actually a virtue—a trait that we should pursue because it leads to life. When we give into our every passion, we make our desires ultimate. Those who are willing to sacrifice their desires are claiming that there is something bigger and better than themselves that is worth living for. In the Bible, that thing is the glory of God.

Read Romans 13:11-14.

What did Paul challenge the church at Rome to do in verse 11?

In what ways might we need to wake up today—particularly with regard to our passions and desires?

These verses help us understand what living in submission to God looks like while not following our fleshly passions. The first thing we have to answer is why did Paul start off verse 13 by saying the words "besides this"? He is referring back to all that he said in Romans 12:1–13:10. In Romans 12:1-2, Paul tells the Christians in the city of Rome to not be conformed to the world but rather be transformed by the renewal of their minds. He is telling Christians to not let the culture shape the way that we think, as how we think determines how we live. This rings true today just as much as it did in Paul's day.

Scan Romans 12:3–13:10. Make a list of how Paul commands Christians to live in these verses.

We can tell whether we are being conformed to the world's way of living or being transformed by the Holy Spirit by looking at Romans 12:3–13:10. Basically Paul says evidence for a life that is being transformed by the Holy Spirit includes: a heart to serve others, walking in humility, not seeking revenge, respecting all levels of authority in our society (e.g., our parents, teachers, coaches, police officers, etc.), and loving our neighbors with the love of God. All of these things can only be accomplished when we are living a life of self-sacrifice.

Our flesh doesn't want to deal with this—it's easier for us to just be quiet and never share the love of God with others. But Paul reminds us that our salvation is nearer to us now than when we first believed. In other words, we must wake up and stop seeking fleshly comfort because we must share the gospel with those who don't know Jesus before He returns. We must live like we know Jesus is coming back. First John 3:3 says, "And everyone who has this hope in Him purifies himself just as He is pure." What this means is, when we live with the belief Jesus Christ is coming back, we will seek to live a pure lifestyle, rather than allowing our decisions to be driven by our fleshly passions.

Given the many outlets in our culture to indulge our passions, how can Paul say that "the night is nearly over" and "the daylight is near"?

What does it mean to discard the deeds of darkness? What might this look like for you?

Take a look at the world around you and you will quickly realize people are living in darkness. The darkest night may be upon us, but with every evening we know that sunrise is coming! Despite the many temptations that surround us, we must not lose hope. We must live like we know that Christ is returning and the best way we can do this is to put on the armor of light.

Paul tells us to discard the deeds of darkness—meaning to give up something and throw it away. To be specific, he is talking about sinful actions. So for those of us who have wrestled with pride, pornography, masturbation, drug abuse, alcohol abuse, and all the deeds of darkness, we must remember that Jesus is our Savior. By looking to Him and relying on the strength the Holy Spirit gives, we can give up these selfish actions. We are to take them off like they are old dirty clothes that we throw in the trash never to wear again. Next, we are told to put on the armor of light, which means to be clothed in light. This is the same process that we discussed earlier about putting on the full armor of God (Eph. 6:10-18).

How can we help one another "walk with decency, as in the daylight" (Rom. 13:13)?

In Paul's writings, when he uses the word "walk," he is specifically speaking about how someone lives—their lifestyle. For Christians, we are to live with clear sight, not stumbling, because the world is watching us. They are watching us because they want to see if our love for Christ is genuine, if our walk really is different from theirs.

So as the world is watching us, they will take notice when we say no to sexual sin, substance abuse, pride, boastful speech, and any other works of darkness they invite us to participate in. A life of self-sacrifice is what many other students in the world you live in are looking for. So while we are living a life of self-sacrifice, we must pray and ask God to give us compassion for the people who don't know Jesus and continually walk in darkness. We need compassion because otherwise we will not succeed in showing them a better way. If we love those who are in darkness, we will help them see the good news that Christ can free them from slavery to their desires. In doing so, we better make sure that we are not giving into the same destructive decisions. If we do, they will rightly call us hypocrites.

This is why we must live in humility, so we can tell those walking in darkness that while we still struggle with sin, we've been restored to God through faith in Jesus' work on the cross. This is how easy it is to share the gospel: Just be transparent about your current struggles and strive to show the people around you the grace God offers us in Christ.

PURITY

Look again at Romans 13:11-14, specifically verse 14. What does it look like to "put on the Lord Jesus Christ"?

A life of self-sacrifice means turning down invitations to go to parties where we know the people will be indulging in anything they want, from alcohol to drugs and sex. A life of self-sacrifice means we will admit when we are wrong and extend forgiveness to those who have wronged us. A life of self-sacrifice means we will no longer desire what others have to the point that we mistreat them because they have what we want. I am talking about their brand of clothes, their better grades, their girlfriend, their starting position on the varsity team, their better chair in band or orchestra, more followers on social media, a bigger house, or both parents in the home. When we give up on our name, reputation, and glory, we will wake up to the reality that Christ is glorious beyond compare and none of these other things will give us the satisfaction our hearts desire.

A life of self-sacrifice means that we put on the Lord Jesus Christ so that our flesh will not drive our decision-making.

A life of self-sacrifice means that we put on the Lord Jesus Christ so that our flesh will not drive our decision-making. Remember Session 1 when we talked about the full armor of God? We talked about the battle gear God has provided for us to put on while we engage in the spiritual war for holy living. We were given that gear by God so we could walk in spiritual victory. Spiritual victory is a reality for all who are clothed in the righteousness of Jesus Christ. So we must put on the armor of light, which is the armor of God, because it is a privilege to be a part of God's army—we are not imposters.

How are we tempted to make plans to satisfy our desires? How is putting on Christ essential to changing these plans?

A military imposter is a person who wears a soldier's uniform in public and makes up stories about experiences in battle, but has never actually served in the military. They exaggerate about experiences they never had. Real soldiers in the U.S. military have posted videos on YouTube when they have confronted a military imposter in public. The real veteran will ask questions about the badges and medals that the imposter is wearing on their uniform. They will ask the imposter to identify the reason why they were given certain badges, stripes, or medals. When the imposter begins to talk, the real veteran will call them out for lying. The veterans then tell the imposters how they are a disgrace to those who are really fighting the war, because they want the glory without the sacrifice of serving.

For the Christian, our testimony of living a life of self-sacrifice is like the genuine badges veterans wear because they earned their stripes in war. When someone comes up to you and starts asking you about your life choices, if you are wearing the full armor of God, you can share your frontline battle stories with them! Explain to them how the power of the gospel frees you to confess your sins and entrust yourself to the Holy Spirit who lives inside of you so that you don't have to be driven by your fleshly passions. Make them aware of the fact that you want to pursue holiness and not physical pleasure every moment of every day. After you have done this, ask them if they want to exchange the deeds of darkness. Encourage them to admit that they are broken and cannot fix themselves and pray that they will cry out to God to be saved through Jesus.

APPLICATION

What does the gospel have to say about our passions? How does the good news about Jesus free us from slavery to our desires?

How does your desire for sex control your thought life? How can you give control of your thoughts back to God?

What steps will you take to stop making plans to satisfy your fleshly desires?

What are three practices you can apply to keep your sinful desires from dictating your decision making?

How might you seek help from a brother in Christ this week in the battle against the flesh? Who do you know who might need your help?

READ

Read Matthew 16:13-28 to get a sense both of how Jesus demonstrated self-sacrifice and how we, like Peter, struggle to understand the value of self-sacrifice.

REFLECT

Why did Peter rebuke Jesus about going to the cross even though he knew that Jesus was the Messiah?

How did Jesus sacrifice Himself for your good? What can you learn from His example?

How might you die to self with regard to your sexual desires? With regard to other selfish desires that are hindering your walk with Christ?

RESPOND

What sacrifices do you need to make in order to get your desires in check? Make a list and spend some time in prayer, asking God to give you the strength you need to make the sacrifices necessary to walk in holiness so that you might treasure Christ and point people to Him.

ENDURANCE

HEBREWS 11:39-12:2

39 *All these were approved through their faith, but they did not receive what was promised,* 40 *since God had provided something better for us, so that they would not be made perfect without us.*

12:1 *Therefore, since we also have such a large cloud of witnesses surrounding us, let us lay aside every weight and the sin that so easily ensnares us. Let us run with endurance the race that lies before us,* 2 *keeping our eyes on Jesus, the source and perfecter of our faith, who for the joy that lay before Him endured a cross and despised the shame and has sat down at the right hand of God's throne.*

WELCOME

Living a life of holistic purity is tough because it takes a lot of energy and commitment. Holy living requires endurance. Perhaps the greatest challenge to endurance is the desire to quit. When you look at our culture, you will notice that we live in a society that is quick to throw things away. Our landfills where garbage collects are flooded with what we think of as trash—things that would be treasures to poorer nations.

We see the evidence of our throwaway culture in the world of entertainment too. Actors and artists often see success early in their careers, but when they fail to follow up with the same or greater levels of success, they are dropped by their record labels and denied roles in blockbuster movies. People in the entertainment industry are here today and gone tomorrow.

▶ PRESS PLAY

Watch the Session 7 video as a group, then discuss the following questions.

DISCUSSION

D.A. said that our culture is a "throw away society." What did he mean by that?

How is Christianity distinct from every other religion? How does this give you hope to endure in your pursuit of purity?

In what areas of your life are you most tempted to give up? How can we encourage one another to endure?

DISCUSS

CULTURE

How do most people today feel about the idea of commitment? What are some examples?

We live in a culture that doesn't value commitment— in particular we don't like to feel tied down. We see this in relationships. A break-up can take place over the smallest argument. Teenagers run away from home when they grow frustrated with their parents. People turn to drugs, alcohol, or even food to comfort them when life gets hard, and they want to escape the pain. Our society loves to tell us we need to change our values regularly. Our culture tells us what's right for today may be wrong for tomorrow, and if we want to be successful, popular, or important we need to conform our values to the culture in order to stay relevant.

The culture tells us if we don't conform, then we will suffer from *#FOMO* (fear of missing out). For example, our culture regularly tells us that rather than sticking with our convictions, we should be curious and explore as much as we want sexually now. Furthermore, according to our culture, we should look into as many religions as possible before we pick one, and if something doesn't work, drop it and move on to the next thing. The world wants you to feel entitled—you should go after whatever you want because you deserve it.

What is wrong with our culture's sense of entitlement—the idea that we should get what we want from life because we deserve it?

Endurance is the ability to make a commitment and stick to it no matter what happens.

Our throwaway culture directly conflicts with the Bible's teaching on endurance. Endurance is the ability to make a commitment and stick to it, no matter what happens. The world encourages entitlement which says, I can have what I want because I deserve it. What the world does not tell us is that every human being, because of our sinfulness, deserves to face God's wrath throughout all eternity! Yet, the gospel tells us that Jesus endured all of God's wrath in full on our behalf.

The Christian life is more like a marathon than a sprint. As a result, we need to work through how to endure in our walk with Christ rather than give into the temptation to quit the race. One of the best passages in Scripture that explains how to endure in our Christian faith while living in a changing world is Hebrews 11:39–12:2.

CHRIST

Read Hebrews 11:39–12:2.

The author of Hebrews says in 11:39, "All these were approved through their faith, but they did not receive what was promised," which causes us to ask, who are the "all these" the author was speaking about? The answer is found earlier in Hebrews 11 with what is known as the Hall of Faith chapter, which is a list of people who trusted in God to be the source of salvation even though they did some crazy, sinful, and messed up things.

> **Briefly look back at Hebrews 11. What were each of the people mentioned in this chapter commended for? Who stands out to you in this list?**

LET'S TAKE A LOOK AT A FEW EXAMPLES:

- **Noah** – In Genesis 6–9 we read the account of Noah's life. He and his family of eight were the only ones God found righteous at the time. As a result, Noah and his family were saved while the rest of the human population was destroyed by a global flood. Yet, we also read that after the flood Noah planted a vineyard, got drunk off his own wine, and did some truly awful things! But as we read in Hebrews 11, although he wasn't perfect, he had faith and he finished his race.

- **Moses** - He is known as the great deliverer of Israel, the nation's leader, the first prophet, and the one to whom God delivered the law. Yet, in Scripture we see that he had serious anger issues that led to God preventing him from entering into the promised land. But as we read in Hebrews 11, although he wasn't perfect, he had faith and he finished his race.

- **David** – He was a man after God's own heart, he slayed the giant Goliath, served as one of the most beloved kings of Israel, and wrote many of the Psalms in the Bible. Yet, he committed adultery, conspired to have Uriah murdered, lied about his sin until he was confronted by a prophet, and failed to discipline his children in critical ways. But as we read in Hebrews 11, although he wasn't perfect, he had faith and he finished his race.

- **Samson** – God raised Samson up to serve as a judge for the nation of Israel and God empowered him to save Israel from the oppression of the Philistines. Yet, we see that he fell into lust regularly, put himself in harm's way, gave away the secret of his strength to a woman who didn't love him, and had his eyes gouged out before he took out a lot of Philistines in a heroic death. But as we read in Hebrews 11, although he wasn't perfect, he had faith and he finished his race.

What temptations most often keep you and other brothers in Christ from finishing the race?

How does humility relate to endurance? If we hope to finish the race, why must we be careful not to become puffed up with pride?

When it comes to sexual sin and biblical characters, it would be foolish for us not to consider this thought: Samson, the strongest man in the Bible; David, a man after God's own heart; and Solomon, the wisest man in the Bible, all fell into sexual sin. We must never think we are smart enough, strong enough, or holy enough to fight off sexual sin on our own. We need the Holy Spirit. We need the Scriptures. And we need the accountability of other brothers, men in our church, to walk with us on the journey of holy living. We must utilize the equipment God has given us if we hope to finish the race. In fact, the word R.A.C.E. can be used to illustrate four crucial aspects of pressing on in our walk with Christ.

R // READ SCRIPTURE

How is studying and applying Scripture essential to staying strong in your walk with Christ?

Reading Scripture helps us to endure because it gives us examples of people who loved God, yet fell into sin, but confessed and finished their race. Romans 8:31-39 is a great passage to read and memorize because it calls us to recognize God's everlasting love for His children. These are the thoughts we must reflect on when we are tempted to quit or think that God is finished with us because we fell into sin again. Those thoughts are from the Enemy of our soul, and he desires to hinder us from finishing our race.

Even though all of the Old Testament saints listed in Hebrews 11 finished their race, they did not receive the promise that we have received They lived in hope of the coming Messiah, whereas we live with the knowledge that the Messiah has come. They awaited the hope of the Holy Spirit—we who trust in Jesus have been given the Spirit.

How do the following Scriptures encourage you to keep following Christ when you are tempted to give up?

- James 1:2-5

- 2 Timothy 3:10-17

- Romans 8:9-16

A// APPRECIATE OUR SALVATION

After we have taken time to read the Scriptures, we must learn to appreciate the salvation that we have in Jesus Christ. Hebrews 12:1 tells us we have a great cloud of witnesses who are cheering us on. One way to picture this is the Olympics. Every four years the Olympic Games are held for which athletes from around the world have been preparing to compete for months and years. One of the most watched events are the races held at night during the track and field segment. The runners line up and compete for a medal. During the race they are cheered on by tens of thousands of people in the stands and billions watching around the world!

How would you feel if billions of people were cheering you on in your walk with Christ? Would it help you endure?

Think about how your adrenaline would be pumping at full capacity with that many people cheering you on. Yet, for the Christian, there is a greater crowd cheering us on in heaven while we are running our race on earth! This truth should challenge us to appreciate the fact that we are not only being cheered on by a great cloud of witnesses, but also that we have the Holy Spirit inside of us who guarantees we will finish our race and cross the finish line into the arms of our Savior!

C// CAST OFF

When we truly appreciate our salvation, we will be motivated to follow the advice of the author of Hebrews who says, "Let us lay aside every weight and the sin that so easily ensnares us. Let us run with endurance the race that lies before us" (Heb. 12:1). To "lay aside every weight" means to remove those things that are weighing us down spiritually, those things that are zapping our energy to effectively run our race. It is important to note that these things are not always sinful, sometimes they are things that we really don't need but are dominating our time and attention.

This reminds me of something that happened back when I wrestled. I had won the state championship the year before and was on my way to defend my title. The first morning of the state tournament, I ate pancakes for breakfast. There's nothing wrong with eating pancakes for breakfast; however, when you are about to participate in a physically grueling sport, pancakes are not the best idea. In my first match, I barely won by a score of 2-0 against an opponent that I had pinned each time I wrestled him before.

After my match, I told my dad I needed to go and lie down because I did not feel well. He told me to get rest because the quarterfinal match would be coming up very soon. As I laid there, I tossed and turned because my stomach was in knots. It wasn't long before I vomited everything I ate for breakfast! A few minutes after leaving the bathroom, my dad ran up and told me they were calling my name, and I needed to report to the mat to compete in my quarterfinal match. I had no energy and strength to compete—I lost the quarterfinal match 13-2. Again, it's not that eating pancakes was wrong, but these pancakes clearly held me back—they were a weight I should have laid aside. This is what the author of Hebrews had in mind. There are things in our lives that are not necessarily sinful, but things that distract us from running the race effectively, things that are weighing us down.

What things in your life might be weighing you down? What would it look like for you to cast them off?

It could be the amount of time we spend playing video games, on social media, listening to music, or watching movies. All of these things may not necessarily be sinful; however, if they are taking up large portions of our time, we're not effectively running our race and living on mission for the glory of God. Then when temptation comes our way, we lack the energy to fight.

Notice how the author says sin "so easily ensnares us." This is because the things that are weighing us down make us an easy target for the Enemy. Living on mission for Christ requires endurance—we build endurance for this race both by growing in faith and by disciplining ourselves. We have to learn to starve ourselves from the things of the world and pray that God would give us a greater appetite for His Word, times of prayer, and times of fellowship with other Christian brothers.

E // ENDURE

Lastly, the best way to endure is simply by enduring! This may sound silly, but think of it this way: the best way to pass in school is to show up to class, do the work that's assigned, ask questions when you don't understand the material, study, complete your homework, and then do the same things the next day. Day after day after day, from August through June, that is your routine. If you do these things, then you will advance to the next grade. A lot of times we know exactly what we need to do, we just need to keep doing those things. So the best way to endure is to simply endure!

This is true in our Christian walk as well. The author of Hebrews says *let us run with endurance*—this simply means a steady determination to keep going and finish the task. This is not a suggestion, but a command, and one that is given with a sense of urgency. The writer is screaming, "Run! Run! Run!" When the world is telling you to quit, or change the course, all the saints in heaven are crying out "Run! Run! Run!"

Look again at Hebrews 12:2. How might "keeping your eyes on Jesus" help you endure?

> When the world is telling you to quit, or change the course, all the saints in heaven are crying out 'Run! Run! Run!

In Hebrews 12:2 the author tells us the best way we can safeguard against straying off course is by keeping our eyes focused on Jesus! We do this by looking at the Scriptures to see how Jesus lived. The Bible tells us in Hebrews 4:15 that Jesus was tempted sin the same ways we are, but He never sinned! He lived the perfect life that we have been unable to live, so He is the perfect model for us to look to for pure and holy living.

PURITY

Read Hebrews 12:1-2 again.

No one can match the example of Jesus when it comes to endurance, so that is why we must continually look to Him in order to finish our race. Not only did Jesus live a perfect life, but He also modeled for us what endurance looks like, even in the face of severe trials and suffering.

How was Jesus able to endure the horror of the cross? What can we learn from His example?

The author of Hebrews tells us that Jesus considered it a joy to endure the cross while being despised and shamed on our behalf. The reason He considered it a chore was because He was fulfilling God's will, so that salvation could be a reality for sinners like us (Eph. 1:3-14). He considered it a joy because He knew He was the only one who could pay the ransom for our sin (Mark 10:45; Heb. 9:15). Lastly, He chose to endure the cross because He would be able to sympathize with us. He understands when we are tempted to quit and walk away from the things of God, but He did none of those things because He finished strong!

> **How might we be more mindful of Jesus and His example of endurance, particularly when we are tempted to quit?**

In a similar way, think about how challenging it would be to learn from and respect a football coach who has never played the game of football in his life. Consider a baseball coach who has never seen a game of baseball, let alone stepped into the batter's box himself. When it comes to the issue of endurance, we do not have a coach who cannot understand what it means to endure—Jesus Christ stepped into our world, put on human flesh like we put on clothes, and lived a perfect life. Then He climbed on a cross and He took upon Himself God's wrath that was due for us. He finished His race and now He gives us the strength to finish ours.

So don't give up! Never stop fighting for purity in your life. When temptation comes and the world tries to distract you from focusing on Jesus, read the Scriptures, appreciate your salvation, cast off the things of the world, and endure! Fight for purity in your thought-life. When it comes to the area of sexuality, walk in purity, and do these same things day after day after day until you see Jesus face-to-face. On that day, you will be like all those mentioned in Hebrews 11, because you will then have finished your race!

APPLICATION

> **How does the gospel give help you run your race with endurance?**

> **What Scriptures could you study and memorize to help you endure in your pursuit of sexual purity?**

> **Do you appreciate your salvation in Christ? How can you be sure?**

> **What are the non-sinful things in your life that you can cast off so that they will not take away your energy to remain sexually pure?**

READ

Read 1 Corinthians 10:1-13. How did most of the Israelites respond to seeing God do great things in their midst? Why do you think they still turned away from God? In what ways are you like the Israelites? What might you learn from their example?

You may not have witnessed the things the Israelites did, but if you've been in church for a while, it is easy to think that you are doing just fine spiritually. In fact, we can become so accustomed to spiritual things that we become complacent. That is what this passage is about. It warns us to be diligent in our pursuit of Christ and in our fight against sin. Ask God to help you run the race with endurance.

REFLECT

What can you learn from the example of the Israelites in verses 1-5? How might you endure where they gave up?

What can you learn from the examples of those in verses 6-10?

How might the promises of verses 12-13 help you endure in faithfulness to Christ when you face temptation?

RESPOND

How will you seek to run the R.A.C.E. (Read Scripture, Appreciate your Salvation, Cast Off, and Endure)? Which of these do you most need to work on? Spend some time praying that the Lord would strengthen you in your area of weakness—ask Him to help you take whatever steps necessary to continue running the race and growing in Christ.

BIBLICAL MANHOOD

PSALM 51:1-13

1 *Be gracious to me, God, according to Your faithful love; according to Your abundant compassion, blot out my rebellion.* 2 *Wash away my guilt and cleanse me from my sin.* 3 *For I am conscious of my rebellion, and my sin is always before me.* 4 *Against You—You alone—I have sinned and done this evil in Your sight. So You are right when You pass sentence; You are blameless when You judge.* 5 *Indeed, I was guilty when I was born; I was sinful when my mother conceived me.* 6 *Surely You desire integrity in the inner self, and You teach me wisdom deep within.* 7 *Purify me with hyssop, and I will be clean; wash me, and I will be whiter than snow.* 8 *Let me hear joy and gladness; let the bones You have crushed rejoice.* 9 *Turn Your face away from my sins and blot out all my guilt.* 10 *God, create a clean heart for me and renew a steadfast spirit within me.* 11 *Do not banish me from Your presence or take Your Holy Spirit from me.* 12 *Restore the joy of Your salvation to me, and give me a willing spirit.* 13 *Then I will teach the rebellious Your ways, and sinners will return to You.*

WELCOME

Throughout our study we have focused on how we can live pure in different areas of our lives. All of the sessions give you a snapshot of what it looks like to live in our world as emerging biblical men. Our world is filled with men; however, not many of them are seeking to live out a biblical worldview that speaks to every area of their life.

Our culture portrays men in many different ways, yet none of them are in harmony with Scripture. On TV shows you will see men who are idiots that only seek to be entertained, who are cowardly and allow women to run their lives, or are addicted to various forms of sexual perversion. In interviews, professional athletes often confess that their definition of manhood was shaped by the men in their neighborhood who were not godly men. They were men who slept with as many women as possible, made money by any means possible, and would physically fight other men in order to prove that they ran the neighborhood. There are many visions of manhood being presented today, but few of them are close to the vision Scripture paints for us. It is time for young men to stop being tossed about by the flow of culture and regain a robust, biblical vision of what it means to be a man of God.

▶ PRESS PLAY
Watch the Session 8 video as a group, then discuss the following questions.

DISCUSS

How are men typically portrayed in the movies and in TV shows you watch?

How does that compare with the picture of biblical manhood D.A. painted for us?

What can we learn about manhood from Jesus' example?

CULTURE

In addition to portraying men as idiots, cowards, and perverts, our culture is constantly telling us that we really never have to grow up. Culture wants us to believe that we can have all the benefits and privileges of manhood without any of the responsibilities that come with it. This is what we call delayed adolescence, which simply means you are no longer a child, but you can keep pushing off being a man as long as you want in order to keep having fun.

Have you witnessed this trend? Have you felt or experienced our culture encouraging you to delay growing up? How so?

What is wrong with this trend?

It's very similar to the story of Peter Pan refusing to grow up. Peter Pan viewed becoming an adult as losing the magic of childhood. Culture is telling you that delayed adolescence gives you the opportunity to choose recreation (fun) over responsibility. This idea develops a work ethic that is poor because it encourages entitlement. Our culture encourages young men to do the bare minimum amount of work while expecting the maximum pay off. Biblical manhood takes work, and it's my prayer that we finish out this series strong by focusing on important keys to live out biblical manhood.

Our world is in desperate need of godly men who will lead with integrity by:

1. Confessing their sins to God.
2. Confronting their shame with the gospel.
3. Modeling compassion to the godless.

Let's take some time to work through these three points by looking at Psalm 51:1-6.

CHRIST

Read Psalm 51:1-6.

From this Psalm, we will unpack three essential qualities of biblical men.

1. BIBLICAL MEN CONFESS THEIR SIN TO GOD AND OTHERS.

When we look at Psalm 51, the first thing we should notice is the introduction that says, "For the choir director. A Davidic psalm, when Nathan the prophet came to him after he had gone to Bathsheba." This Psalm was not originally written for private meditation or reflection rather, it was written and delivered to the chief musician for the public reading and singing throughout the entire nation of Israel.

What had David done that he needed to confess to God and repent of?

This entire Psalm is King David's confession of sin! He is literally telling the entire nation of Israel that he is repenting for the sins he committed, specifically adultery and murder. Biblical men understand that there are consequences for our sins, and sometimes they will last for years after we have confessed, repented, and received forgiveness from God regarding them. There is beautiful freedom in confessing our sins to God. However, because we live in a fallen world, not all of the consequences for our sinful actions go away even though God forgives us.

> There is beautiful freedom in confessing our sins to God.

I think back to a few years ago when I was dropping my oldest daughter off at school. At the time, she was 10-years-old and as I was pulling up to the parking lot at her school to drop her off when she looked at me and asked, "Daddy, were you a virgin when you married mommy?" My heart stopped as soon as she asked me. I had a limited amount of time to answer, but I needed to answer her with honesty. I looked her in the eyes and solemnly told her the truth, I was not a virgin when her mom and I got married. I told her I was not a believer, and I lost my virginity during my early teenage years. I told her that I did ask Jesus for forgiveness, and I asked Elicia to forgive me for not entering into our marriage sexually pure, and she forgave me as well.

How does David's prayer differ from the way men tend to apologize when they are caught in adultery?

Seeing the disappointment in her eyes, I told her that at the time I did not think one day I would have to explain to my daughter that I was not a virgin when I got married. I told my daughter I was ashamed of my actions. She forgave me and told me she loved me. I told her that virginity is a precious gift that we only give away once and I encouraged her to learn from the consequences of my sin and the embarrassment that still comes with it even though I've been forgiven. I then challenged my daughter to save herself sexually until her wedding night, to avoid the same embarrassment when her child asked if she was pure when she entered into the covenant of marriage.

As young men being introduced to the topic of biblical manhood, never forget that there are consequences for your actions in your teenage years that could last for the rest of your life. Let this help to motivate you to say no to sexual temptation and yes to purity!

2. BIBLICAL MEN CONFRONT THEIR SHAME WITH THE GOSPEL.

If there is a time when you face the consequences for sinful actions like I did when my daughter asked about my virginity, remember to confront your shame with the truthfulness of the gospel message.

How did David confront His shame with truth about God (see Ps. 51:1-2)?

In Psalm 51:1-2 David said, "Be gracious to me, God, according to Your faithful love; according to Your abundant compassion, blot out my rebellion. Wash away my guilt and cleanse me from my sin." Here we see King David recognize that his sin made him guilty. He cried out for God to have mercy on him, which means he was begging God to have compassion on him regarding his sinful actions.

In the Hebrew language, David used an impersonal term for God. This was the first time he referred to God this way in the psalms. Normally he spoke of God in a personal and intimate way. Think of it this way: normally we do not refer to our parents or guardians by their first names when we speak to them. We use more intimate terms like "dad/mom," "grandpa/grandma," and "aunt/uncle." We rarely call them Mr. or Mrs. Now imagine you did something hurtful on purpose to disappoint your parents or guardians and were convicted of your sinful actions. If you began to distance yourself from your parents by avoiding them, what would it say to them if you addressed them as Mr. or Mrs.? They would probably be insulted because you are family—not some stranger you address formally.

In a similar way, this is what David was doing to God. He knew he was guilty and felt ashamed because of his sinful actions. He referred to God like a stranger—he felt distant from God because his sin made him feel unworthy of even mentioning His name. Although David felt this way, he did not continue in this thought for very long. He overcame his shame by crying out to God for forgiveness and remembering God's steadfast love.

David knew God keeps all of His promises, and he asked God to remember His promise to have unfailing love toward those who have a covenant relationship with Him. David knew he could not earn this love because he did not deserve it, and the gospel tells us the same. We should have a similar thought like David did of God during those times that we feel guilt and shame for our sin. We may feel like we should not get too close to God because of our moral failures; however, His love reminds us that we can come to Him at any moment of any day to receive grace and forgiveness in our time of need.

What did David ask God to do in verse 2?

Why is it crucial for us to not constantly dwell on the shame of our sin? How does this contradict the gospel?

David then asks God to "blot out my rebellion. Wash away my guilt and cleanse me from my sin." In his request, David understood that God is the only one who can completely wipe away all of our sins. The gospel reminds us that it is the shed blood of Jesus that washes away sin, and those of us who have embraced Christ as Lord and Savior have had our guilt removed through Jesus' shed blood (Heb. 7:26; 10:12-14). Even though David knew his sin separated him from a holy God, he knew that God would be willing to cleanse him so he could be used again by God for His service.

This reminds me of a time when I stayed the night at my older brother's house shortly after he and his wife got married. I was around 13-years-old and my brother was in his early 20s. I stayed up really late and got hungry. I went into the kitchen and fixed myself a pot of Cream of Wheat (a hot cereal made on the stove). After eating the cereal, I forgot to wash out the pot and the leftover residue became cold and stuck to the bottom of the pot.

In the morning, my sister-in-law went into the kitchen to make breakfast and found the dirty pot on the stove. When she realized the pot she needed to make breakfast had not been washed, she got upset and asked me to wash it. Cleaning the pot was challenging because I had to get hot water in another pot so it could soak in dish soap for about 15 minutes. Then I had to take a stainless steel pad and scrub the pot for about five minutes. After the process was over, it was clean and able to be used again.

In a similar way when we sin and neglect to confess it to God, it's like that cream of wheat. Our heart gets cold. But then when we hear the gospel message of the forgiveness that God extended to us and cry out to Him, He begins to scrub us. Like that pot, God scrubs out our fleshly guilt and shame. And then when the process is complete, we can be used by God for the intended purpose that He has for us. Biblical men confront guilt and shame from the consequences of their sin with the gospel. This process reminds us that God is not finished with us; He wants us to endure for His glory!

3. BIBLICAL MEN MODEL COMPASSION TO THE GODLESS.

In Psalm 51:3-5, we see David taking ownership for his own sinfulness. This is something biblical men must learn to do consistently. We must learn to admit when we are wrong, take ownership for our sinfulness and our mistakes, and ask for forgiveness from those that we have sinned against.

How could David say "against You—You alone—I have sinned" when he had also sinned against Bathsheba, Uriah, and the people of Israel?

David recognizes that although other people were affected by his sin, the first person that he sinned against was God. Biblical men recognize the first person we should confess our sinfulness to is God, and after we receive forgiveness from Him we should then go to those we've sinned against to confess our sin and seek forgiveness. When other people come to us seeking forgiveness, we must remember how God has graciously forgiven us. Biblical men extend the same compassion to others they have received from God.

As we seek to be biblical men, why is it important that we remember that we, like David, were born in sin?

David also recognizes that his sinfulness has been with him since he was in his mother's womb. Biblical men recognize that we were born dead in sin. This truth helps us recognize that we are prone at any time to fall into any sin. The culture tries to tell us it's easier to say we are sick rather than saying we are wrong. This is why our world needs biblical men to step up and admit our sin and live in transparency.

For I am conscious of my rebellion, and my sin is always before me. Against You—You alone—I have sinned and done this evil in Your sight. So You are right when You pass sentence; You are blameless when You judge. Indeed, I was guilty when I was born; I was sinful when my mother conceived me.
—Psalm 51:3-5

PURITY

Read Psalm 51:13. How might practicing confession and repentance prepare us to impact others?

Here we see David, who has been forgiven from his sins and has received the joy of his salvation once again (as he states in Ps. 51:12), now admit that he is a qualified candidate to show sinners what forgiveness from God looks like. This is the truth biblical men operate under on a day-to-day basis. God has called every Christian to proclaim the gospel, and who better to proclaim the good news that sinners can be forgiven from sin than those whose slate has been wiped clean by the blood of Jesus!

Then I will teach the rebellious Your ways, and sinners will return to You.
—Psalm 51:13

No matter where God sends you, never forget the gospel message as you strive to live in purity in every area of your life. If you ever find yourself wrestling with guilt and shame because you have fallen into sin and you are scared to confess, read all of Psalm 32 and recognize this is the torture David put himself through when he refused to confess his sins to God. After you have read Psalm 32, read Psalm 51 and make it your prayer as you confess your sins to God.

Biblical men are not perfect, but we strive to walk in purity. Biblical men recognize the only way we can walk in holistic purity is to understand that the gospel reminds us our identity is found in the work of Jesus Christ, not in what we have done or what we have:

- Remember forgiveness and redemption have come through the shed blood of Jesus Christ, not by any of our works.

- Demonstrate God's love to our brothers and sisters in Christ by protecting their hearts and putting to death our fleshly desires.

- Walk in humility that gains the attention of God, and once we have His attention we walk in obedience to His commands found in Scripture.

- Daily practice self-sacrifice by not allowing fleshly passions to determine the decisions we make in life. Rather, we allow God the Holy Spirit to give us the strength to say no to sin and yes to holiness.

- Endure by reading Scripture, appreciating the salvation we have in Jesus, and casting off the things that weigh us down and cause us to fall into sin.

Holy living in the area of sexuality is possible for every Christian. Do not fall for the lies of the world telling you it's impossible. God the Holy Spirit lives inside every Christian, and He gives us the strength to fight our flesh every moment of every day. The greatest decision you can make every moment of every day is to say "yes" to the leading of God the Holy Spirit and "no" to the desires of your flesh. If you do this on a consistent basis, you show the world the beauty of how true love waits for the time God has determined for it to be awakened.

APPLICATION

What is a gospel-centered definition for manhood?

What are some areas you need to grow and mature in?

Biblical men confess their sins and endure their consequences. How has the material we've worked through encouraged you to confess and endure the consequences of your sinful actions?

What are some ways you can show compassion toward others in your home, school, and student ministry?

READ

Read Psalm 1 and make a list of ways you might strive to cultivate a more biblical vision for manhood from this text. According to this Psalm, what does a biblical man look like? How does a biblical man live? What practices does he engage in throughout the week?

REFLECT

What does the Psalmist warn against in verse 1?

What does he encourage us to do in verse 2? What would this look like for you?

What is promised to those who obey the commands of verse 2 (see v. 3)?

How might the truths found in verses 4-6 help us fight temptation and pursue purity?

RESPOND

Now that you have come to the end of our study on personal holiness, take some time to take a spiritual inventory of your life.

Has your perspective on sex, purity, or manhood changed since the beginning of this study? How so?

What principles from this study have you put in place as a means to grow in holiness?

What principles do you still need to put into practice? What steps will you take to do so?

LEADER
GUIDE

First of all, thank you for your commitment to lead guys through this study! We are praying for you and want you to know you are not alone in this. Thank you for giving of your time and of your resources to serve guys and to point them to Christ. Our hope and prayer is that they will understand God's love for them in Christ and that they will daily offer their bodies as living sacrifices to Him.

HOW TO LEAD A GUYS' BIBLE STUDY

Whether this is your first time or your 50th time to lead a guys' Bible study, we want to help you guide the guys in your group through God's Word. The videos are an important component, so try to designate at least 10-12 minutes for viewing the videos from D.A. at the beginning of each session.

We've included the *Main Point* of every session at the beginning of the following Leader Guides, as well as some *Leader Prep* helps. Do not feel bound to covering all of the options and questions included in the Leader Guide, simply use it as a guide.

Get Started will give you some tips for opening the session. This is also a good time to recap the previous session and introduce what will be covered in the current session as well. Then you will *Press Play* and watch the video for the session you are in, and that should be followed up with discussion.

There are a few different ways you can approach the *On Your Own* section. For most groups, it will be best for guys to take their books home to complete this section during the week. If you do conclude the session early though, go ahead and give guys the opportunity to complete this at the end of the session.

TRUE LOVE WAITS HISTORY AND INFO

About twenty years ago a small group of students in the Nashville area committed themselves to Christ in the pursuit of purity, not knowing that thousands of additional students would join them. This movement came to be known as *True Love Waits*.

Over the years *True Love Waits* has witnessed hundreds of thousands of young people commit their sexual purity to God, while offering the hope and restoration in Christ to the sexually broken. It has been a tremendous movement, orchestrated by God, to spread the biblical message of sex and purity to a younger generation.

There is a Commitment Card in the back of this study that you can use with your group. Remind guys that this is a serious commitment to personal holiness. Don't pressure your students to make this commitment, but use this as a tool to generate conversation and lead your students to embrace the power of accountability in their pursuit of Christ through Christian community.

To purchase additional commitment cards, see *lifeway.com/truelovewaits*.

Most of your the guys in your group probably play video games or at least have played video games in the past. Video games often allow us to create our own character and assign points to the character's attributes. For instance in a football game, you would assign points to your character's speed, agility, throwing, or catching abilities. Keeping this in mind, what would you say are the attributes of living a holy life? What characteristics or virtues must we max out if we hope to live a pure and holy life pleasing to God? In this session you will give an overview of seven attributes or virtues essential to living a holy life. In the sessions that follow, you will lead guys to examine the world and the Bible's definition of the following virtues: identity, redemption, love, humility, self-sacrifice, endurance, and biblical manhood.

- Prior to your meeting read through Session 1, highlighting and taking notes on what you want to cover with the guys in your group during this session.

- During this study, guys will be challenged to acknowledge that God calls them to be holy and to begin taking steps toward growing in purity as young men of God.

Introduce yourself and briefly get to know the guys in your group. If you know in advance that there are a lot of guys in your group who do not know each other, you might want to play some sort of icebreaker activity to allow them to get to know each other better. One way you could do that is with the following activity:

Tell the guys in your group that you need their help designing a video game character for Madden (a football video game). Let them choose what to name the character and what position he plays. Tell them that they have 100 points to assign to the following attributes: strength, speed, agility, stamina, injury resistance, throwing strength, throwing accuracy, catching ability, jumping ability, elusiveness, tackle breaking ability, tackling, coverage, and awareness. Let students argue a bit about what attributes they think are most important to the particular position your character plays. After they have allotted all of their 100 points, ask them what they think are the most important attributes of a holy life.

PRESS PLAY

Set up and make sure the video system is working in advance so that it is ready for you to simply press play. Watch the Session 1 video (included in the DVD Kit). Allow time for discussion after. There are discussion questions on page 9 specifically designed to go along with the Session 1 video.

DISCUSS

This time of discussion will build on the video guide discussion on page 9. Dive into the topics and themes that were introduced in this session's video and build your conversation around these topics and questions.

- **CULTURE:** What does our culture say are the most important attributes of a successful life?

- **CHRIST:** In contrast to this, what does Scripture say? What are the attributes of a holy life?

- **PURITY:** What does "sanctification" mean? What are some practical ways you might grow to be more like Jesus?

ON YOUR OWN

This section is designed for guys to complete at the end of your meeting if time allows. If you are pressed for time, encourage the guys to complete this section during the week as they reflect on what they have studied so far. Suggest that they find somewhere quiet where they can spend time with God thinking about and processing what it means to live a life of holiness.

FOLLOW-UP

Consider compiling a contact list and use it to keep in touch with the guys in your group this week. Set up a group message or email where you can remind them of truths from this week's session and send reminders about your next meeting.

NOTES

SESSION 2: IDENTITY

MAIN POINT

This session will help guys understand their identity in Christ as children of God. We will examine who our culture tells them they need to be vs. who God says they are in Christ. Students will be challenged to reject the world's definition and make every effort to root their identity in Christ.

LEADER PREP

- Prior to your meeting briefly look over Session 1 before reading through Session 2. Highlight and take notes on what you want to cover with the guys in your group during this session.

- During this session, guys will be challenged to acknowledge who God has made them to be, how sin has wrecked us, and how Christ offers to renew and restore us to be the men God created us to be.

- Prior to your meeting, place signs around the room where you will be meeting with the following words written in large letters on them: Student, Son, Athlete, Friend, Church Member, Band Member, Gamer, Reader, Artist, and Leader.

GET STARTED

To begin your study, instruct the guys in your group to go stand by the sign with the title they most identify with or that best describes how they see themselves. Once they are done, tell them that we are going to compare and contrast the identity that our culture ascribes to students today with the identity Scripture gives to followers of Christ. Help students to see that while each of these titles may identify them on some level, there is a far more important and far deeper identity that God gives to everyone who trusts in His Son.

PRESS PLAY

Set up and make sure the video system is working in advance so that it is ready for you to simply press play. Watch the Session 2 video (included in the DVD Kit). Allow time for discussion after. There are discussion questions on page 19 specifically designed to go along with the Session 2 video.

DISCUSS

This time of discussion will build on the video guide discussion on page 19. Dive into the topics and themes that were introduced in this session's video and build your conversation around these topics and questions.

- **CULTURE:** What are some of the "hats" you wear (i.e., son, student, church member, basketball team member, band member, etc.)?

- **CHRIST:** Rank the various "hats" you wear in terms of their importance. What's wrong with placing any of these "hats" above the our ultimate identity as children of God?

- **PURITY**: How might misunderstanding your identity affect your pursuit of purity?

ON YOUR OWN

As guys complete this section at the end of your group time or on their own, challenge them to be honest with the Lord about their insecurities and weaknesses. The first step to rooting your identity in Christ is to see how you don't have it all together. You need Jesus. Encourage guys to spend some time in prayer acknowledging this and admitting their need for Christ.

FOLLOW-UP

Send a text this week to your guys with 1 Peter 2:9-10. Challenge them to memorize these two verses and to remember who they are in Christ.

NOTES

SESSION 3: REDEMPTION

MAIN POINT

While the culture we live in sees forgiveness as limited and dependent, we serve a God who offers us forgiveness that is full and free. In this session, students will unpack how the promise of redemption in Christ frees them from the enslaving power of impurity and empowers them to become more like Christ.

LEADER PREP

- Prior to your meeting, review Session 2 before reading Session 3. Highlight and take notes on what you want to cover with the guys in your group during this session.

- During this session, guys will discover Scripture's definition of forgiveness and be challenged to walk in the power of knowing they are fully and finally forgiven through Christ.

- Before your group meeting, search the Internet for "famous apologies." Find a few notable ones that the guys in your group might be familiar with that were made by politicians, celebrities, or other famous athletes. Consider printing these out and bring them to your group meeting.

GET STARTED

Hand out the famous apologies to your students. Assign one student to each and have them share with the rest of the group what that apology consisted of. Ask the other students in your group whether they think it was a good apology or not. Ask them whether most people who heard this apology accepted it or not and whether or not forgiveness was truly achieved.

Talk to students about how unforgiving our culture can be. No matter how remorseful or repentant someone is, our culture does not forget. People might claim to have forgiven a celebrity or an athlete for doing something wrong, but they will not forget. In fact, the second that person does something wrong again, our culture will remind us of their past failures and mistakes. In this session, we will see that the forgiveness God offers is not like this. In Psalm 103:11-12, the Psalmist says that God removes our sins "as far as the east is from the west." In other words, when we truly cry out to God for forgiveness and trust in Christ, He determines to never throw our past mistakes in our faces. He chooses to no longer hold them against us.

PRESS PLAY

Set up and make sure the video system is working in advance so that it is ready for you to simply press play. Watch the Session 3 video (included in the DVD Kit). Allow time for discussion after. There are discussion questions on page 29 specifically designed to go along with the Session 3 video.

DISCUSS

- **CULTURE:** By the world's definition, how is forgiveness always a gamble?
- **CHRIST:** How is forgiveness guaranteed in Christ? How can you be sure you have been forgiven of your sins?
- **PURITY:** How should we respond when we begin to feel the conviction of sin? How should knowing that Christ has redeemed us encourage us to live a pure life?

ON YOUR OWN

As guys complete this section at the end of your group time or on their own, challenge them spend some time dwelling on the fact that the penalty of sin is death, yet God chose to impose that penalty on Jesus instead of them. Encourage them to write out a prayer to God, thanking Him for the full and free forgiveness He provides in Christ and praying that His forgiveness would empower them to grow in holiness.

FOLLOW-UP

As a means of following up on what students learned, text them the following question, "What is the difference between godly sorrow and worldly grief?" If they don't know the answer, text them 1 Corinthians 7:10 and remind them that worldly sorrow refers to being upset that you got caught or upset about the consequences of sin. Godly sorrow involves the brokenness that comes from knowing that you have sinned against God and longing for a closer relationship with Him.

NOTES

SESSION 4: LOVE

MAIN POINT

Our culture says that as long as we let people have what they want, give them space to enjoy what they have, and never tell them their desires are wrong, then we love them. In contrast, Scripture calls us to love others like Christ loved us by giving Himself up on the cross for us. True love is humble, self-sacrificing. If you truly love someone you will point them to the only one who loves perfectly—Jesus Christ.

LEADER PREP

- Prior to your meeting, review Session 3 before reading Session 4. Highlight and take notes on what you want to cover with the guys in your group during this session.

- In this study, you will challenge students to see the destructive nature of the world's definition of love. Consider some examples from your own life when you thought of love in primarily selfish ways. How has your perspective on love changed since you became a Christian? Sharing a personal story of how Christ has changed your perspective will drive home the main point of this week.

- Look up some popular love songs prior to your meeting. Find some that are appropriate for your group to discuss and print them out and bring them to your group meeting.

- Find some advertisements in magazines or online that have the word "love" in them. Make sure they are appropriate for you group, cut them out or print them out and bring them to your group meeting.

GETTING STARTED

As you begin this session. Assign one group to read through the song lyrics and another to look through the advertisements. Ask the song group to share with you what their songs say about love. Ask them how these songs define love and how they think that might compare with Scripture's definition of love. Ask the advertisement group the same questions.

PRESS PLAY

Set up and make sure the video system is working in advance so that it is ready for you to simply press play. Watch the Session 4 video (included in the DVD Kit). Allow time for discussion after. There are discussion questions on page 39 specifically designed to go along with the Session 4 video.

DISCUSS

- **CULTURE:** What is our culture's definition of love? What is wrong with thinking of love primarily in selfish terms?
- **CHRIST:** How has God shown you His love? How does Jesus demonstrate God's love for us?
- **PURITY:** How might a less selfish and more Christ-like view of love change the way you treat girls?

ON YOUR OWN

Guys will be challenged to read Ephesians 5:22-33. As they do so, encourage them to see that while this text is about marriage, it still has much to say to them about how they should live now as single young men. If husbands are called to love their wives like Christ loved the church, that means single students should constantly strive to honor the women in their lives rather than use them for their own pleasure. Ask students to honestly consider whether they've seen girls in their school, neighborhood, or church in unbiblical or selfish ways. Challenge them to repent of such attitudes and commit instead to honoring them and treating them with dignity and respect.

FOLLOW-UP

Send an email or text this week reminding students of what love truly is according to 1 Corinthians 13:1-7 and challenging them to continue repenting from a primarily selfish view of love.

NOTES

SESSION 5: HUMILITY

MAIN POINT

We live in a culture that sees the pursuit of personal greatness as a given and even encourages students to go to great lengths to attain it and keep it. Christ calls us to a better way. Rather than constantly trying to prove how great we are, Christ calls us to declare spiritual bankruptcy—to admit that we do not have it all together and confess our desperate need for Jesus. It is only when we see our own need that we will look to Christ for help and position ourselves to love and serve others in humility.

LEADER PREP

- Prior to your meeting, review Session 4 before reading through Session 5. Highlight and take notes on what you want to cover with the guys in your group during this session.

- In this study, students will be challenged to let go of any feelings of self-sufficiency that they have and open their eyes to how desperately they need Jesus. Once students see that they are spiritually needy and that Jesus has served them by giving up His life for their sins, they will then see how Jesus calls them to serve others.

- Search for the best or funniest humblebrags on the internet. A humblebrag is a statement that is made to sound humble or modest, but actually serves to draw attention to something the person making the statement is proud of. Find several that are appropriate for your group—they could be tweets or YouTube videos. If using tweets, print them out, and if they are videos, prepare a way to show them to students at the beginning of your meeting.

GETTING STARTED

Ask students to define the word "humility." Once you've come up with a working definition as a group, show them some of the examples of humble brags that you found. Don't explain what a humblebrag is, just show students the examples and then ask them whether they think these are examples of humility. Help your guys to see that pride is an enemy to faith. We live in a culture that is constantly encouraging us to stoke our pride—to think we are great and to even come up with ways to prove or convince others of our greatness. The humble brag is the perfect example. Athletes, politicians, and celebrities constantly use the humble brag so that they won't look prideful while still telling everyone how great they are. The gospel, however, paints a different picture. In today's session we will see that on our own, we are not great. True greatness is found when we see how much we need Jesus. When we see our need for Jesus, we will stop living for ourselves and instead live to glorify God by loving Him and serving our neighbors.

PRESS PLAY

Set up and make sure the video system is working in advance so that it is ready for you to simply press play. Watch the Session 5 video (included in the DVD Kit). Allow time for discussion after. There are discussion questions on page 49 specifically designed to go along with the Session 5 video.

DISCUSS

- **CULTURE:** D.A. said guys are "fixers that don't like failure." How have you seen this play out in your life?
- **CHRIST:** Despite what our culture says, God is not impressed by our greatness. Those who are humble, who see their need for Jesus, have the special attention of God.
- **PURITY:** Thinking too highly of yourself leads to impurity and compromise. Don't make the mistake of thinking you can handle temptation in your own power. Challenge students to think of ways they can commit to living in purity by relying on the strength God gives and by looking to their brothers in Christ for help.

ON YOUR OWN

At the end of this session, if time permits, lead guys to spend some time reflecting on the areas of their lives in which they are self-reliant. Challenge them to confess these things to God and ask Him to help them rely less on themselves and more on Christ.

FOLLOW-UP

Text Philippians 2:3 to your students and follow it up with the following question: Who will you consider more important than yourself this week? What will you do?

NOTES

SESSION 6: SELF-SACRIFICE

MAIN POINT

Our culture responds to our sexual urges by giving us many different outlets to exercise them and ways to try and avoid the consequences of doing so. Self-control is not popular in our culture. In fact, among many young people today, it is just assumed that you will experiment sexually before marriage. Scripture, however, tells us that true satisfaction can only be found when we let go of our selfish desires and live for something bigger than ourselves, namely the glory of God and the kingdom of Christ.

LEADER PREP

- Prior to your meeting, review Session 5 before reading through Session 6. Highlight and take notes on what you want to cover with the guys in your group during this session.

- In this study, students will see how the world wants our passions to control our decision making process. Christ offers us true freedom—the power to control our passions with the help of the Holy Spirit.

GETTING STARTED

To open your time with your students this week, choose two or three of the following scenarios and ask students what would be required in order to achieve these things:

- Become a professional athlete.

- Become a millionaire.

- Become President of the United States.

- Have a happy and committed marriage.

Successfully achieving any of these goals would require sacrifice. To become a professional athlete would require refusing to eat what everyone else eats and to spend your time the way everyone else does—you would be forced to sacrifice your time and attention and energy if you wanted to achieve this. The same is true of these other things as well. Anything that you want to do well is going to require sacrifice. This is certainly true of your walk with Christ. If you want to live for Christ and His kingdom, you need to start thinking now about what He might be calling you to sacrifice in order to live a life of purity that positions you to glorify Him in all that you do.

PRESS PLAY

Set up and make sure the video system is working in advance so that it is ready for you to simply press play. Watch the Session 6 video (included in the DVD Kit). Allow time for discussion after. There are discussion questions on page 59 specifically designed to go along with the Session 6 video.

DISCUSS

- **CULTURE:** How does our culture encourage young men to respond to their passions and desires?
- **CHRIST:** True joy and true satisfaction does not come by giving in to our impulses, but by controlling them and directing them according to God's will. How did Jesus demonstrate this for us? How did His sacrifice lead to joy?
- **PURITY:** What might God be calling you to sacrifice in order to live a life of purity?

ON YOUR OWN

Close out your time with your students with some time of silent reflection. Ask them to close their eyes and bow their heads and think about what in their life might be keeping them from living a life of purity? What might God be calling them to sacrifice in order to better glorify Him?

FOLLOW-UP

Text Matthew 16:24 to your group this week with the following question, "What will you sacrifice this week in order to follow Jesus and pursue purity?"

NOTES

SESSION 7: ENDURANCE

MAIN POINT

We live in a throw away culture—today everything is expendable. Don't like your job, your school, or your team? Just quit. This is why so many marriages end in divorce and why so many young people are afraid of commitment. We need something bigger than ourselves to live for. Thankfully the gospel provides just that. The gospel opens our eyes to see that we were made to live for the glory of the God who made us and loves us. Living for Christ in a throwaway culture, however, is difficult because the world around us is constantly telling us to quit. In humility and with a willingness to sacrifice ourselves for Christ, we must endure.

LEADER PREP

- Prior to your meeting, review Session 6 before reading through Session 7. Highlight and take notes on what you want to cover with the guys in your group during this session.

- In this study, students will be challenged to see through the lies of our throwaway culture and endure in their pursuit of purity.

- Prior to your group meeting, search the Internet for stories of "Famous Quitters." Find a story or two that are appropriate for your group, print it out or save it on your phone to share with your group at the beginning of your meeting.

GETTING STARTED

Share a story of a famous quitter with your group, then ask the following questions:
- Why do you think this person quit?
- What kept them from enduring?
- How did their quitting affect the people around them?
- What would you have done differently?

PRESS PLAY

Set up and make sure the video system is working in advance so that it is ready for you to simply press play. Watch the Session 7 video (included in the DVD Kit). Allow time for discussion after. There are discussion questions on page 69 specifically designed to go along with the Session 7 video.

DISCUSS

- **CULTURE:** We live in a throwaway culture that is afraid of commitment. This shows in our relationships, our work, and our friendships. Be prepared to talk about some examples of our throwaway culture with your group.

- **CHRIST:** Christ is fully committed to those who trust in Him—He promises to never leave or forsake them.

- **PURITY:** Jesus' endurance in loving and saving us is a picture of the kind of endurance we must strive for if we hope to live lives of purity. Where are you struggling to endure? When are you most tempted to quit?

ON YOUR OWN

Give each student in your group a sheet of paper or a notecard and a pen. Instruct them to write "R-A-C-E" on their sheet. Next to each letter, they will write one way they might strive to live out the letter represented in order to run the race of purity with endurance this week:

- **R /** Read Scripture
- **A /** Appreciate your Salvation
- **C /** Cast Off
- **E /** Endure

FOLLOW-UP

Send texts throughout the week encouraging your guys to run the R-A-C-E with endurance this week.

NOTES

SESSION 8: BIBLICAL MANHOOD

MAIN POINT

Pop culture portrays men in many different ways but few of them are positive. Rather than bumbling idiots, big kids, or irresponsible deadbeats, Scripture calls men to be humble, compassionate, and Christ-like leaders. In a culture that tells boys they don't have to grow up, we desperately need to regain a biblical understanding of manhood.

LEADER PREP

- Prior to your meeting, review Session 7 before reading through Session 8. Highlight and take notes on what you want to cover with the guys in your group during this session.

- In this study, students will regain a biblical understanding of manhood. They will see that true manhood is strong but also compassionate—biblical men model Christ's compassion to the godless. Biblical men are confident in Christ but also humble. They confront their shame with the gospel.

- Prior to your meeting, print out or save on your phone or tablet pictures of prominent men in culture and history. Bring these pictures to your meeting. Examples could include presidents, movie stars, rappers, athletes, and pastors.

GETTING STARTED

To begin your study, show the pictures of prominent men to your students. After showing each picture, ask your students the following questions:

- If we based our understanding of what it means to be a man on this person, what would we conclude?

- What is admirable about this person's portrayal of manhood?

- Do you see anything problematic about this person's portrayal of manhood? How so?

PRESS PLAY

Set up and make sure the video system is working in advance so that it is ready for you to simply press play. Watch the Session 8 video (included in the DVD Kit). Allow time for discussion after. There are discussion questions on page 79 specifically designed to go along with the Session 8 video.

DISCUSS

- **CULTURE:** A lot of men today suffer from "Peter Pan syndrome"—they don't want to grow up. Are there areas of your life where you are tempted to give into this way of thinking? In what aspects of life do you not want to grow up?

- **CHRIST:** Christ is the ultimate example of biblical manhood. In everything Jesus did, He modeled for us what it means to live in purity for God's glory. What have you learned from Christ's example in terms of how you understand and live out manhood?

- **PURITY:** Holy living in the area of sexuality is possible for every Christian! Do not fall for the lies of the world that tell you it's impossible. Look to Christ for the strength and direction you need.

ON YOUR OWN

Encourage students to read Psalm 1 and make a list of ways you might strive to cultivate a more biblical vision for manhood from this text. What according to this Psalm does a biblical man look like? How does a biblical man live? What practices does he engage in throughout the week?

FOLLOW-UP

At various points throughout the week, text the response questions to your students:

- What principles from this study have you put in place as a means to grow in holiness?

- What principles do you still need to put into practice? What steps will you take to do so?

NOTES

By the time you have reached this section, you have hopefully gone through all eight sessions of *Authentic Love.* It is our hope and prayer that by this point, the words on this commitment card are an accurate reflection of where your heart is right now in regard to your commitment to Christ in your pursuit of purity.

truelovewaits.
COMMITMENT

In light of who God is, what Christ has done for me, and who I am in Him, from this day forward I commit myself to Him in the lifelong pursuit of personal holiness. By His grace, I will continually present myself to Him as a living sacrifice, holy and pleasing to God.

Signature _____

Date _____

NOTES

NOTES

NOTES

NOTES